The Orphan
How One Man Innovated His Village Against All Odds

ALEJANDRO ARDILES CAJA

The Orphan

How One Man Innovated His Village Against All Odds

ALEJANDRO ARDILES CAJA
1918-2018

Julia Ardiles de Espinoza

DEDICATION

I dedicate this book with infinite love to my three wonderful children—Dianna, Karina, and Pedro David—for being my most demanding students and teachers at the same time, and to all those who read it. I hope it inspires you to fulfill your dreams.

 **100% of proceeds will go to panperu.org**

Pan Peru is a 501(c)3 nonprofit organization that empowers women, children, and the environment by building multimedia libraries, executing reforestation programs, and empowering underserved females to become entrepreneurs. Pan Peru was founded in 2004 by engineer Julia Ardiles de Espinoza with the vision to foster and promote education in one of the least developed nations of Latin America.

www.panperu.org

ACKNOWLEDGEMENTS

Above all, I thank God the Lord Jesus Christ for making this book possible.

I thank my husband, Pedro Espinoza Orihuela, for giving me my three greatest blessings—my children.

To my mother, Victoria Fortunata, thank you for your prayers.

I thank my nine loving siblings—Marcela, Ángel, Elena, Alex, Bernabé, Edith, David, César, and Carlos—for their constant support and for sharing their experiences and testimonies.

Finally, I thank Martín Lúcar Figueroa, Reynaldo Trinidad, Hugo Aguilar, Lucio Cevallos, my aunts and uncles, nieces and nephews, and everyone that has contributed in one way or another to this work.

INDEX

	MESSAGE FROM THE AUTHOR	16
01	Between the Sea and the Sky	17

- THE BOY THAT BECAME THE MAN OF THE HOUSE
- A DIFFICULT CHILDHOOD
- DEATH AND LIFE IN THE POWER OF THE TONGUE
- IN CONQUEST OF LIMA
- SUCCESS COMES FROM HARD WORK, NOT HANDOUTS
- THOSE WHO LOVE TO WIN LOVE TO PLAY
- GOD ACTS WHEN MAN NO LONGER CAN

02	Everyone Returns To Their Homeland	35

- ENTREPRENEUR
- LIFE BECOMES A UNIVERSITY WHEN WE MEET A GREAT TEACHER
- LOVE AND MARRIAGE
- WHAT DO YOU DO WHEN YOU LOSE A LOVED ONE?
- CHAMPIONS START WHERE THEY ARE WITH WHAT THEY HAVE

03	A Sleeping Businessman Inside Us All	45

- A LOVING BROTHER
- THE LEADER BREAKS NEW GROUND
- THE RICH MAN'S GOATS
- AN UNWAVERING WORKER
- HONESTY WAS HIS GREATEST FORTUNE
- ROCK SOLID CHARACTER
- HE WAS HARDWORKING AND PERSEVERING
- A GREAT SPEAKER

- INTELLIGENT
- A DANCER
- THE ORPHAN THAT INNOVATED HIS VILLAGE
- GROWING HIS TERRITORY

04 How He Innovated His Village   63
- VISION
- A PIONEER IN WORKING WITH FERTILIZERS AND INSECTICIDES
- DON ALEJANDRO'S TIE-WEARING COWS
- AN EARLY RISER
- A GOOD APPRAISER
- IN CONTROL
- HE TURNED CHALLENGES INTO OPPORTUNITIES FOR GROWTH
- QUILLCÁN—HEAVEN ON EARTH
- AN EXCELLENT HUNTER
- UNFORGETTABLE NIGHTS IN QUILLCÁN
- FIVE "HUACHACAZOS"
- AN OUTSTANDING MAN
- POTATOES WITH VITAMINS A TO Z

05 He Served In Politics Without Pay   81
- GOVERNOR OF PAMPAS
- DON ALICHO AT CITY HALL
- HIS MASTERPIECE
- HE PROMOTED SPORTS IN PAMPAS

06 A Rigorous Spiritual Life and a Happy, United Family   89
- HIS WIFE—HIS IDEAL HELPER
- EDUCATION—THE BEST INHERITANCE
- HOW HE TIGHTLY UNITED HIS FAMILY
- PERU, THE CHAMPION!

07 On Being a Good Father — 101
- TOUGH LOVE
- A PRESENT FATHER MAKES EXCELLENT STUDENTS
- HE PROTECTED HIS CHILDREN'S SELF-ESTEEM
- HE LOVED AND PROTECTED HIS CHILDREN
- HE MOTIVATED HIS CHILDREN
- WHAT HE DID WHEN HIS CHILDREN GOT BAD GRADES
- HE PRAISED HIS CHILDREN'S ACCOMPLISHMENTS
- HUG EACH OTHER! KISS EACH OTHER!
- HOW HE RESPONDED TO TANTRUMS
- HE TAUGHT HIS CHILDREN TO BE RESPONSIBLE
- HE TRIED TO AVOID SAYING "NO"
- HE HAD FAITH IN PEOPLE
- HE LIMITED ELECTRONIC USAGE
- HE MADE TIME FOR EACH CHILD
- HE TAUGHT HIS CHILDREN NEVER TO GIVE UP
- HE INSTILLED SELF-CONFIDENCE IN HIS CHILDREN
- HE CORRECTED WISELY
- HE NEVER LIED TO HIS CHILDREN
- HE INDULGED HIS CHILDREN
- A LEADER SEES THE BEST IN HIS CHILDREN

08 An Exemplary Citizen — 123
- A SERVANT
- HE DIDN'T MINCE WORDS
- HE GAVE BREAKFAST TO ORPHANS
- HE PROMOTED SOLIDARITY AFTER THE 1970 EARTHQUAKE

- HE APPEARED ON TV AND THE COVER OF A MAGAZINE ASKING FOR AID FOR HIS VILLAGE
- HE BROUGHT TECHNOLOGICAL ADVANCEMENTS TO PAMPAS GRANDE
- HE EMPOWERED LOCAL FARMERS
- HE UNITED TWO TOWNS
- HIS FAMOUS SPEECH
- HE PROMOTED LOVE FOR HIS HOMELAND
- HE PROMOTED THE CONSTRUCTION OF THE HIGHWAY BETWEEN PAMPAS AND LIMA

09 Final Goodbyes   139
- FUNERAL EULOGY TO DON ALEJANDRO ON THE DAY OF HIS PASSING, MARCH 12, 2009

10 Alejandro Ardiles Caja's Massive Legacy   143
- ALEJANDRO ARDILES CAJA'S LEGACY

APPENDICES

Ardiles Aniceto Family Tree   146

Testimony of His Children   150

Testimony of His Family and Friends   160

Stories   164

Photographs   168

PROLOGUE

Reading *The Orphan*, so aptly and readably written by one of his daughters with heartfelt testimonies from people who knew don[1] Alejandro Ardiles so well, is like stumbling upon a refreshing oasis in the middle of the desert. I believe that because, in a day and time where corruption, selfishness, and lack of respect for others rule, it is both encouraging and inspiring to learn of the struggles, victories, and massive contributions of a brave man that impacted and blessed the lives of so many.

When we read the headlines of the newspapers, listen to the news on the radio, or see pictures of what is happening in our cities, our countries, and in the world, we see only the bad, and it makes us more and more pessimistic about the future, but Alejandro Ardiles Caja's life brings hope back into our hearts. It makes us realize that if this could happen to a humble boy from a district known as Pampas Grande—"a balcony hung between the sea and the sky" in the Huaraz province almost 12,000 feet above sea level in the Andes mountains—, the same things could happen to others deciding to live according to God's purpose in their lives.

One of the greatest lessons that "Alicho," the protagonist of this story, leaves us is that being born in a humble home, losing his father at the age of nine, suffering the humiliation of returning to his grandparents' home as a servant in exchange for a bowl of "watery soup and corn kernels," being confined to the service area of the house despite being a

---

[1] 'don' is an honorific for men and 'doña' is the female equivalent

legitimate grandson, and later working like a slave at a rundown chifa[2] joint with no pay or tips just to survive were not reason enough to fill his heart with resentment and bitterness and, like so many, end up resentful or as a delinquent.

Neither did he allow discrimination and mistreatment to crush his deepest dreams and desires. He did not succumb to self-pity or to low self-esteem, instead overcoming and triumphing in life in every sense of the word. Just like the apostle John wrote to his good friend Gaius, "… I pray that you may enjoy good health and that all may go well with you, even as your soul is getting along well" (NIV).

This brings us to the other great lesson that I see in this true story: success in life is far more than simple economic prosperity. It has to do with living with faith, love, and the fear of the Lord, which makes us lead a life of dignity, values, love and respect for our neighbors, and, finally, purpose. In doing so, we can "transcend and leave a legacy." This is the desire that the author expresses to her readers as well as my own desire upon finishing the prologue to the book. Based on that desire, I can highly recommend this book.

Pastor Humberto Lay
Former Commissioner on the Truth and Reconciliation Commission,
Congressman for Lima

---

2   A Chinese-Peruvian style restaurant common in Peru

MESSAGE FROM THE AUTHOR

This book is based on the life of Alejandro Ardiles Caja, or "Alicho," and its aim is for the reader to be able to see the infinite power of God, who is faithful to those who love and obey him. Alejandro Ardiles Caja was tireless in his fight to help both his family and his town progress. Throughout his life, he faced many difficulties, and even though it seemed like he was destined to fail or to be just another face in the crowd, he overcame his difficult circumstances and always ended up successful.

What was his secret? He practiced daily that which God requires of humanity—he defended justice, gave to the poor, took in strangers, cared for the afflicted, was an exemplary father, and had a deep love for his people. That's why God rewarded him just as the Holy Scriptures say:

> And the Lord will guide you continually and satisfy your desire in scorched places and make your bones strong; and you shall be like a watered garden, like a spring of water, whose waters do not fail.
> —Isaiah 58:11

Alejandro grew up and lived in the face of adversity. He was an orphan with scarce resources and education and a neglected farmer. However, he ultimately became the highest authority in his town, the best farmer and herder of Pampas Grande, a pioneer, leader, visionary, athlete, the head of a unified family, and loved and respected by those who knew him. His slogan was, "Go with God!"

This book's aim is to inspire readers with the life of Alejandro and to motivate them to fulfill their dreams, overcome their circumstances, and to leave a legacy.

Love,

Julia Ardiles de Espinoza

Pampas Grande before the 1970 earthquake. On the right is the San Jerónimo school shortly after its opening in 1965.

01

BETWEEN THE SEA AND THE SKY

There was once a man named Alejandro Ardiles Caja. Adults called him "don Alicho," but kids just called him "Uncle Alicho." He was born on May 3, 1918 in the picturesque Pampas Grande district (in the Huaraz province of the Ancash department of Peru). Of German descent, he was the firstborn of don Bernabé Ardiles Robles and doña Elena Caja Dyer.

Back then, Pampas Grande was known as the "balcony hung between the sea and the sky" due to its peculiar geographic features and strategic location. It sat among what seemed like unscalable mountains where condors, hawks, sparrows, and butterflies flew. It was incredible! All at the same time, you could see the tallest mountains in Peru (Huascarán with its white peaks as well as Huandoy) and, in the evenings, the most beautiful sunset over the sea as if you were sitting on a celestial balcony. At night, you could almost reach out and touch the sky with all its stars.

Pampas Grande was a lovely village with cobbled and raised streets, a majestic colonial street with two huge bells, and houses with adobe roofing, red tile, and raised chimneys for venting the smoke from cooking over wood. Every morning, you could hear the chickens clucking and the pichusancas chirping.

Alejandro's birth caused a stir in the Ardiles family because their parents didn't approve of doña Elena. She was the single mother of little Gregorio—the child of her first love. Back then, the Ardiles family thought very highly of themselves due to their fair complexion, blue or green eyes, and the Quillcán estate (a Quechua[1] word meaning "where there is silver"), which was two and a half hours outside Pampas. Their ostentatious houses even had hanging gardens and their tables boasted fine linen tablecloths. They only used stoneware and chinaware and their many servants waited on them respectfully. The ladies used elegant French perfumes and never went unnoticed. When they had exclusive visits, it was only from clergy or the highest officials, which is exactly why they felt so offended by Bernabé's "misstep" of falling in love with Elena, whom they looked down upon even though she was good-looking, hard-working, and good-natured.

Bernabé's parents having rejected their marriage, he and Elena were staying with his uncle Juan Ardiles Robles and doña Paciencia Dextre, who also had a son named Juan. Alejandro would develop a close bond with this cousin, who was about his same age and to whom he gave the nickname "Juancucho." They would remain brothers and close friends into their old age.

In spite of these circumstances, little Alejandro had a happy childhood along with his little sisters Laura and Antonieta. He was a mischievous and lively child. With his rosy cheeks and dark brown hair blowing in the wind, he would often play with his cousins on the hillside of Quillcán. He and his cousins in the Ardiles family—the children of his father's eight siblings who lived on the estate—played ball, spin-a-top, hide and seek, and any other game that came to their heads.

They went to bed with the sun and woke up to the rooster's crow every day because they had to do everything during the day. At night, only lamps or kerosene lanterns lit up the area like stars. On nights with no moon, there was total darkness and Alejandro would take a candle in his small hands to stay out just a little longer.

---

1 Quechua is the indigenous language spoken in parts of Peru, Bolivia, and Ecuador

A magnificent sunset from Pampas Grande (the balcony between the sea and the sky). Below, clouds cover the ocean and Pariacoto while the peaks of Bom Bom are peeking through.

The place where he grew up was very bucolic—the flora, fauna, fields, livestock, and mountains were all there was. Roads, motorized vehicles, running water and drainage, electricity, radio, internet, television, and telephones didn't even exist in their dreams.

Pampas Grande enjoyed mild weather. It frosted in the mornings and at night, but also got very hot during the day. Since bacteria dies in the heat and in the cold, the Peruvian saying, "When the sun's here, the doctor isn't" always came true in Pampas Grande.

Mail only came by postillions or mule drivers that carried letters by foot and packages by donkey. It took so long that when people got sick, people only knew after they were either healthy again or dead.

Alejandro started school at the 335 Boys School in Pampas Grande at the age of six. Back then, the teachers dressed up in suits and ties and even wore vests and golden watch chains. Every morning, they taught the students strict rules of civility, discipline, and hygiene, and the students had to wear military uniforms with caps and ties. They were required to train every morning before starting the school day. The education was so good that they learned in one year what they now learn in three. The school brought the students up with strong values, starting with respect for their neighbors and love for their country. The lessons were clearly visible in the way that they said "Good morning" or "Good evening" every day. It was, without a doubt, a golden age, especially for Alejandro Ardiles, who didn't know how much was about to change.

335 Boys School in Pampas Grande where don Alejandro was a student.

THE BOY THAT BECAME THE MAN OF THE HOUSE

Alejandro's life changed suddenly when don Bernabé, his father, died of a severe colic. Alejandro, Laura, and Antonieta, who were nine, six, and one years old respectively, were orphaned.

At this young age, little Alejandro, with tears in his eyes and newfound responsibility, had to become the man of the house. His paternal family, who had rejected his father, didn't take compassion on the three orphans, which made their childhood very difficult. In third grade, Alejandro had to leave school and work very hard to support his mother and sisters.

Alejandro, Laura, and Antuca[2] were seen as the "ugly ducklings" of the Ardiles family, so their mother, doña Elena, decided to move back to her birthplace—the town of Succha in the Aija province—with all her children. It was a challenging journey, and they had to go over the dangerous icy puna[3] alone, risking encounters with pishtacos[4], bandits, and raiders that would steal animals and even slit their victims' throats. To combat his fears, **Alejandro folded his hands and prayed** whenever he thought he saw a pishtaco. God heard him, and they safely arrived in Succha. Unfortunately, doña Elena was rejected for the same reason. They only found refuge for his half-brother Gregorio, who stayed with his uncle Jacobo Fernández Caja and would later move to Huarmey to live with him.

Doña Elena and her three younger children had to trek back across the mountains weighed down by fear and lack of food. When they got back to Pampas Grandes, the Ardiles family took them in as mere servants and gave them only watery soup and corn kernels to eat, never even allowing them to enter the living rooms of their houses.

---

2   A nickname for Antonieta
3   A rugged plain found in the Andes mountains
4   A Peruvian folkloric character that captures and murders travelers

The Pampas Grande church bells rang daily at school time.

A DIFFICULT CHILDHOOD

In the midst of these difficult circumstances, a talkative Chinese immigrant who would bring about great change in the life of our protagonist suddenly appeared in Pampas Grande. He came from the Huarmey port, which, according to him, was all sunshine and rainbows, and he made thousands of promises to doña Elena so she would let her son go and work with him as an altar boy or a priest's assistant. He promised her anything in exchange for her approval, and he finally got it. She built up the courage, blessed Alejandro, and let him go, all the while begging God for his safekeeping.

The Chinese man had tricked her, and Alejandro had hardly set foot in Huarmey when he made him a "chulillo," which was the lowest servant status. He forced Alejandro to work in a run-down chifa restaurant and nicknamed him "Giveaway."

While there, he had to work many different jobs from carrying buckets of water on his shoulders to carrying charcoal, peeling potatoes, slaughtering ducks or guinea pigs, washing plates, mending clothes, cleaning floors, ironing, cooking, shining shoes, and waiting on tables, which he did without pay or tips—all for a little food to eat and a run-down place to sleep.

"Don't be a coward you giveaway! Stop crying!" the Chinese man would yell at him in a heavy accent as he looked from a distance at the donkey they used to collect trash. "Straighten up and get back to work!"

Pain tends to be an excellent teacher for those who are ready to overcome it. Alejandro **trusted that God was protecting him**, so he kept folding his little hands, looking up to the sky, and praying, which is how, by some miracle, he met don Emiliano Servat—the brother-in-law of his uncle Isaías Fourier, the husband of Alejandrina Ardiles—in Huarmey.

Young Alejandro looked up to don Emiliano for being a loving father who fought to keep his ten children unified and happy, always saying that "the best inheritance children can get is an education." Years later, don Emiliano would build a house in Lima's Miraflores district and go there to live with his family. Alejandro also saw that don Emiliano was a hard worker who had two estates—one for livestock and the other for agriculture. He planted in large quantities and sold his products in Lima.

Don Emiliano would come to be his mentor, and Alejandro remembered all the positive things that he heard and saw there.

Alejandro lived in Huarmey for almost four years completing various difficult tasks. However, one day, he had a horrible accident. He was trying to light the Primus stove at the chifa joint when a flame licked his face.

"The Serranito[5] burned himself!" everyone yelled while running about.

---

5 Serranito refers to someone who comes from the mountains

Alejandro leapt in pain until someone ordered them to put sea lion oil on the wound, which worked wonders. He recovered without scarring, but he knew that it was really the power of God helping him!

After recovering, he escaped back to Pampas Grande with the help of his big brother Gregorio. Even though this was a difficult period, the backbreaking work helped develop his abilities and grit. At a young age, he knew how to do a bit of everything—even swim and play soccer. Unintentionally, the charlatan, exploitative Chinese man had prepared him for life.

> "And we know that for those who love God all things work together for good"
> —The Apostle Paul

DEATH AND LIFE IN THE POWER OF THE TONGUE

Returning to Pampas Grande, he found his mother engaged to a day laborer named Lorenzo Salas with a child of the same name. Lorenzo's strict example helped Alejandro develop a rock-solid backbone. He harangued Alejandro daily and taught him lessons that he would never forget:

Get up early and quick!

There's no place for laziness here!

Let's go! Stand up straight!

Rain or shine, hot or cold, don't be lazy!

You're a good kid! You're young!

Don Lorenzo encouraged him daily, giving him courage and determination and teaching him to rise early, work hard, and be dedicated.

Alejandro learned these lessons well and practiced them for the rest of his life.

Years later, his mother, her husband, and Lorenzo Junior moved to the town of Quian at the head of the Culebras valley in Huarmey. Her daughters Laura and Antonieta went to live with their aunt Beatriz Ardiles and her husband don Heraclio Castillo, and her oldest went to their aunt and uncle Isaías Fournier and Alejandrina Ardiles de Fournier. Isaías was the son of a French landowner, and he taught him secrets of raising livestock. He also took him to visit nearby farms like Chacchán and Colcabamba in the Casma River basin. These experiences shaped Alejandro's personality and perspective made him an early riser and a hard worker, winning his aunts' and uncles' admiration.

Being agile, he learned to tame wild bulls by doing pirouettes with his waist. He was also a fine hunter. He hunted doves, deer, partridges, and vizcachas with his uncle Isaías.

> "Death and life are in the power of the tongue,
> and those who love it will eat its fruits."
> —Proverbs 18:21

IN CONQUEST OF LIMA

In 1935, when Alejandro was 17 years old, he accomplished a lifelong goal—stepping foot in Lima for the first time. After saying goodbye to his mother and receiving her and his sisters' blessings, he left with his uncle Julio Ardiles Robles and his cousin Juancucho, promising to come back to his family.

Today, the trip from Pampas Grande to Lima takes about 8 hours. Back then, it took them more than three months. They went on foot and horseback to Huarmey, then by boat to Callao, and then by train from the port to Barrios Altos, where his uncle Julio's cousin Jose Ardiles lived.

After arriving, they decided to walk to his uncle Jose's house, but the summer sun in Lima quickly wore them out. They tried to hail a taxi several times, but the drivers passed them by when they saw how ragged they looked.

The first picture taken of Alejandro Ardiles. He had honey color eyes and dark brown hair.

"Go take a plaza car!" the drivers yelled.

Then they would innocently ask, "But how do we get to the plaza to take one?"

Finally, a driver felt sorry for them, parked, got them into the car, took a few turns, and charged them fifty cents. It was the same price they would paid from the start since they had only gone two blocks.

Lima, the City of Kings, held many new sights in store—crystal clear pools, colonial-style mansions, and organized public transit with shiny new cars. They were tired, happy, and hopeful when they arrived. They walked upright and their boots clapped heartily against the street. They were the nicest shoes they had ever owned—the shoes they wore to fulfill the dream of every country boy back then: to visit Peru's capital city.

Alejandro and Juancucho fantasized about a dignified future—getting a good job and maybe even wooing some cute Limeñas by offering them the "high life." ("At 12,000 feet above sea level in Pampas Grande, that is," they would say while laughing).

SUCCESS COMES FROM HARD WORK, NOT HANDOUTS

However, it wasn't easy in Lima. They faced the same hardships and disappointments as every other country person who came to live in the capital, and they understood the courage and dedication necessary to start something from nothing.

After considerable effort and with recommendations from their uncle Julio, they started working as helpers to bricklayers and cart drivers. Day after day, they sweated under the weight of heavy carts filled with sand and crushed rocks and barrels filled with water and bricks over their shoulders. Their hands cracked and they suffered through extreme heat in the summer and humidity in the winter, but they weren't discouraged. On the contrary, they gathered the strength to carry on.

> "A slack hand causes poverty,
> but the hand of the diligent makes rich."
> —Proverbs 10:4

THOSE WHO LOVE TO WIN LOVE TO PLAY

The work days seemed endless and the only things that kept them going under the weight of cement were their dreams and their newspaper hats protecting them from the sun. They were paying rental fees for a Lima flat that they crushed under their destroyed boots.

Don Alejandro was a huge soccer fan. Below are his sons Carlos, Bernabé, and Alex.

Alejandro, always having been disciplined and mature, never wasted time on vices like alcohol, which was very common among bricklayers, and even convinced Juancucho to play soccer on the weekends.

He fell in love with soccer, starting with a ball made out of rags on improvised pitches with no goal posts, boundary lines, or referees—just rocks as a goal and white chalk to mark off the pitch. Around the same time, the National Stadium was being built. They were fascinated by the project, so they used to play around the construction. While playing, they learned to work as a team, to value friendships, to be disciplined, to listen, and, above all, to understand that there are days when you win with humility and others when you lose with respect.

Alejandro kicked hard and did somersaults when he scored. Playing soccer, he recovered his self-esteem.

> "Sports change your mind, heart, and even your life for the better."
> —Lionel Messi

GOD ACTS WHEN MAN NO LONGER CAN

On a normal work day at 19 years of age, Alejandro received a devastating letter.

"Your mother has gone to be with the Lord, and your sisters are alone with four more orphans: Gregorio, Lorenzo, Moisés, and Rebeca."

What was he, a poor day worker in Lima, to do about his now completely orphaned sisters? He felt sad, alone, and abandoned.

He kept working, nobody noticing that he was suffering the most intense pain of his entire life. He lost his appetite, got sick, and had to be admitted to the Workers' Hospital. Under a pavilion packed with the sick, **he once again turned to God** and faithfully prayed for help. "God never fails!" he thought. **He knew that no problem was too big for God.**

After recovering, he became even more methodical and decided to save money for emergencies, to eat better, to take naps on cement bags after lunches, and to keep exercising. This decision would make him an attractive, strong, and confident young man.

His new lifestyle allowed him to save 200 soles[6], which he invested in a business with his older brother Gregorio. Unfortunately, the business failed, but he wasn't discouraged. He learned that businesses only prosper when you personally care for them. He thought, "If you want something done right, do it yourself," so he kept working and investing his profits.

While doing this, he learned to become a contract bricklayer instead of simply being a bricklayer's assistant. He was eager to succeed, and he learned to fill trenches to make the base for walls, lay down stem walls, and place formwork with sand, crushed stone, and cement. Later, he learned to make iron columns with exact measurements, which he easily memorized, and to use plumb lines—using a pendulum to measure the verticality of the wall and making a precise calculation to plaster it evenly. He also mastered finishing columns with more elevated styles of molding, which were made 13 feet high in colonial style high relief.

---

6   The Peruvian currency

By working punctually and responsibly, Alejandro became a successful bricklayer and surpassed others who had started long before him, earning not only their respect, but also that of his engineer bosses.

As master builder, he made more money, which motivated him. He told himself, "I'll make more and save more, then start my own business!"

His older brother Gregorio with his son Julián and his nuclear family in Huarmey, 1982.

"There is a driving force more powerful than steam, electricity, and atomic energy: the will."
—Albert Einstein

Pampas Grande's cobbled streets.

02
EVERYONE RETURNS TO THEIR HOMELAND

Alejandro returned to his beloved Pampas Grande and, from then into his old age, would never stay away from it for very long. He would regularly travel to different parts of his country and others to learn, but always returned to his people with innovations and improvements.

Don Alejandro still didn't know that his return was the best possible decision. Life would undoubtedly be different without his mother, but he could also again see his sisters—now grown into beautiful women. Laura was 21 years old and married to Braulio Yauri Alegre. His reunion with her was moving. They shared the emotions, tears, and warm embraces over their reunion and the memories of their mother's passing. On the other hand, Antonieta was a beautiful sixteen-year-old young woman who hardly remembered her mother after having been separated from her as a child. Her honey-colored eyes filled with tears as she smiled joyfully—the family was back together, crying tears of joy.

His sister Laura Ardiles Caja.

"Alicho, you're finally back!" said Antuca.

"Our parents Bernabé and Elena down on us seeing us together again!" added Laura.

"They sure are, so we need to stay together from now on." added Alejandro.

And so, for the rest of their lives, they stayed close to each other and left that legacy to their children and grandchildren.

ENTREPRENEUR

Twenty-four years old and supporting himself on his savings, Alejandro asked himself, "Who will I be? How will I go farther?" and, "What businesses can I invest in?" Being very observant, he concluded that a liquor store would succeed in Pampas Grande, where, one could traditionally occasionally go without water, but never without liquor.

After working in construction in Lima for seven years without days off or frivolous spending, he started his first business. His initial investment was in the Central Market, where he bought liquor wholesale, then transported it by truck to Huarmey, and then to Pampas Grande on pack animals. It was a nearly month-long endeavor of walking through abandoned, steep, beaten-down paths; however, he went along singing and whistling. During torrential rains, he put on a poncho, prayed in silence, and was confident that God went with him, which calmed and strengthened him.

"Let's go! Let's go!" he would prod his donkeys.

His intelligence and hard work paid off. He opened his store in the heart of the Pampas Grande Plaza de Armas and enjoyed success from day one. That business became the staging area for endless stories, experiences, and nights of talking. He learned many jokes there that he would tell for the rest of his life—he had an excellent sense of humor and was always cheerful, jocular, and excited.

His nephew remembered, "When drunk men stayed into the night instead of going home to rest, Don Alejandro would make fun of them by selling them their own urine as if it were beer. He could never tell those stories without cracking up."

Wanting to continue working as a master bricklayer in Lima, he became the first person in Pampas Grande to create jobs by hiring personnel from the town to work in his store while he worked in Lima. Without realizing it, he had set the wheels of progress in motion in his community.

> "Have I not commanded you? Be strong and courageous. Do not be frightened, and do not be dismayed, for the Lord your God is with you wherever you go."
> —Joshua 1:9

LIFE BECOMES A UNIVERSITY WHEN WE MEET A GREAT TEACHER

When he returned to Pampas Grande, he stayed with professor don Bruno Valverde Granda, who was a great teacher and the husband of Alejandro's cousin Zoraida Alegre Ardiles. It was strange to meet a college graduate in a small town, and stranger still that he was as patient, kind, and loving as don Bruno. It was surely God who put him in Alejandro's path.

Don Bruno became his educational mentor, teaching him the importance of treating children well and not making them cry, scaring them, or discouraging them. He also taught him not to say "no" without reason, to never lie to them, and to set a good example and praise them. Later, Alejandro would put all this advice into practice with his own children

At the opening of the San Juan school. In yellow is don Bruno Valverde. Among others are his cousins Lidia Ardiles and Cesario Trinidad.

and grandchildren. In doing so Mr. and Mrs. Valverde Alegre lovingly contributed to Alejandro's own education by teaching him values.

The years spent going between Pampas Grande and Lima were hectic. He brought his sister Antonieta during one of his trips, hoping to find a better future for her. With Alejandro's blessing, she married don Porfirio Valenzuela, a responsible young man with whom Alejandro would form a lifelong friendship. This was one of the best times in Alejandro's life—he was happy, healthy, and living up to his potential.

> "Whoever walks with the wise becomes wise..."
> —Proverbs 13:20a

LOVE AND MARRIAGE

She was hardly seventeen and Alejandro was twenty-six. It was love at first sight, just like in the movies. Alejandro recalled, "It was a chance encounter. I was in San Juan visiting my sister when I saw her for the first time. I smiled and tried to talk to her, but she told me no, 'some other time.' I went again the next Sunday and found her. I told her, 'I like the dimples in your sweet face and your braided black hair.' She smiled and blushed, and that's how our love began that spring."

A beautiful evening view from the Plaza de Armas in Pampas Grande.

They met in secret because doña Filberta Alegre, Victoria Fortunata Aniceto Alegre's mother, was very strict. She was so concerned about keeping her kids busy that she would throw bean and barley seeds on the floor and make the kids separate them. On occasion, when she left the house, she would pay their neighbor don "Oso Domingo" to chase her children back to her house spanking them if he saw them playing in the street.

"Yes ma'am, doña Filberta. I sure will!" He would say.

Obviously, with such a strict mother, it was nearly impossible for Victoria Fortunate to fall in love—much less find a husband. She hardly had any opportunities to form friendships with anyone. When she saw don Alejandro, however, her fear of her mother was dwarfed by her attraction to him.

Alejandro called her "Oto," and they had a lovely relationship. He would sing "Cry, Cry, My Heart[7]" to her.

You are the waves,
and I am the beach.
You come to me, you caress me,
you kiss me once, then you leave.
Cry, cry my heart!
Cry if you want to go back!
For it's no crime for a man to cry
if he cries for a woman

One day, Fortunata built up the courage to talk with her parents.

"Mom, I want to marry him."

"No way, sweetheart. No way. Men are liars—my first husband left me with your brother Braulio and the second one left me with Margarita."

"But you had four kids with my dad."

"I got lucky with him up until now. But it's better if you don't get married. You're a cholita[8] from the country—he'll just take advantage of you."

So, when Alejandro went to San Juan to propose, he got a negative response.

---

7   "Llora, llora, corazón" by Luis Gálvez Ronceros
8   A term used to describe a young girl descended from indigenous peoples in the Andes

"Mánan[9]!" they told him.

They decided to run away together in 1945. Just like a fairy tale, they had their honeymoon under the countless stars in the night sky. When doña Filberta learned of the marriage, she had no choice but to accept it, so she gave them a place in her house in San Juan that her husband don Marcos had built.

Being an honorable and hardworking man, Alejandro won his in-laws' respect quickly. Fortunata had strong principles and values, was industrious like her mother, and was selflessly dedicated to her family, which is why, upon hearing of the marriage, uncle Isaías Fournier Ardiles said, "Alicho made a perfect choice!"

> "Love is the best motor for development."
> —Anonymous

WHAT DO YOU DO WHEN YOU LOSE A LOVED ONE?

Every winter, fog covered the ground like a blanket at Pampas Grande, trapping the frozen air. However, when the sky cleared, you could see the Pariacoto Valley below as well as the road that cut through it.

Life is sometimes like that too—we're surrounded by difficulty like a thick, dark gray fog that the sun can't penetrate. However, faith is the best way to lift yourself out of the valley.

---

9   The Quechua word for 'No'

Alejandro and Fortunata faced a difficult test when their firstborn, Victoria Elena, who was already walking, passed away at the age of one due to an issue with her stomach. They had patiently waited for her. She was a happy girl—the fruit of the love they had for each other—and she had her whole life ahead of her, but God had other plans.

They wept bitterly, and **they begged God** to never take another child away from them. They closed their store for a week and promised to serve him and stay faithful forever. Only through faith in Him were they able to overcome the darkness and gain a new perspective in life.

> "...seek the things that are above..."
> —Colossians 3:1

CHAMPIONS START WHERE THEY ARE WITH WHAT THEY HAVE

One day, doña Filberta came to their house to visit them.

"What's this, mom?" asked Fortunata.

"They're a gift, sweetheart. Just like your family grows with children, your flock can only grow with hard work."

"Thank you, mama. What are their names?"

"This calf is Flor de Habas and that one is Neblina"

In that instant, Alejandro, who was a visionary, saw himself as a great breeder in the future; so, driven by his desire for success, he began to grow his livestock by trading his bull calves for other farmers' heifers. With just those two calves, he began breeding in San Juan with no idea that he would become the best breeder in the region.

03

A SLEEPING BUSINESSMAN INSIDE US ALL

Anybody can become a businessman when they have an entrepreneurial spirit. Don Alejandro once pitched a new business idea to his wife:

"We could make a lot of money working on other farms. If they put in their land and the seeds and we put in the work, we could split the crop 50/50 with the owners. Then, we'll eat what we need and sell the rest. When we have enough capital, we can buy our own farms! I can mortgage those farms to the bank for a loan and make bigger investments. With God's help, I know we'll go far."

"That sounds great, Alicho," his wife wisely responded.

Just like that, Alejandro started cultivating potatoes, wheat, and barley.

Later, he started another new business—a hog farm. The pigs multiplied quickly and he fed them using the extra barley that he grew.

The hardest part was walking the herds to Pariacoto—where the road passed through—where he would load to pigs into trucks and take them to Huacho to sell them.

During this trip, he would have to sleep outdoors with no cot or blanket while caring for his animals, which could escape or be stolen. He also had to take care of the donkeys that carried the barley to feed the pigs—counting and recounting them and catching the ones that escaped. They also carried "colchados," which were mats made out old wool bags that traders used to sleep in while on the road.

He fed his pigs with his own barley harvests.

To avoid that hassle, Alejandro moved his hog farm from San Juan to Pashicuta, which is closer to Pariacoto, where the animals could drink from a crystal-clear stream, find shade under lush trees, and eat to their heart's content. These changes lowered the cost and increased profits. With the business well under way, he hired farm hands to work on the hog farm while he kept alternating between his business in Pampas and his contract bricklaying in Lima.

His in-laws' support was instrumental for him because he was able to leave his wife and children, who were being born about every two years in San Juan, in their care. He frequently traveled to Lima for building contracts where he bought merchandise to supply his store in Pampas, which was now full steam ahead.

The downside to these trips was that his children were born while he was away, and there was no way of keeping in touch. His father-in-law, don Marcos, gave Alejandro's kids ridiculous names that he found in the Bristol Almanac[10] (like Theodosia, Urban, Restituta, and Purification), which, fortunately, Alejandro later changed to more common names.

---

10   El Almanaque de Bristol is a Spanish language almanac that has been published continually since 1832

A LOVING BROTHER

Around that time, don Braulio Yauri Alegre, the brother of his wife Fortunata and husband of his sister Laura, passed away. Don Braulio left four orphans: Roman (8), Guido (6), Delfín (4), and Clotilde (2). Again plunged into grief, the family used this trial to grow their faith in God. His intelligent and hardworking sister Laura developed virtues, and don Alejandro and doña Fortunata were supportive in helping raise her children as their own.

His sister Laura's children Coty, Violeta, Delfin, Roman, Hugo, Guido, Judith, and Laura Juanita—all current US citizens.

One day, their nephews Guido and Roman decided to play a trick on their aunt.

"Aunt Fortunata! Get up! Earthquake!"

Doña Fortunata, feeling her cot shaking, starting praying in her bed, "Hail Mary, full of grace..."

Her nephews started cracking up—the bed was shaking from the dog happily scratching itself below after having eaten the leftovers of a ham the two boys had just mischievously devoured. It was a model family, and they joked and played together with complete trust. Alejandro loved his two sisters dearly and was a father to his orphaned nephews—correcting them and making them do their homework.

Toya, the daughter of his sister Antonieta, was beautiful and thin, but suffered from many allergies in Lima: sinusitis, pharyngitis, tonsillitis, rhinitis, and bronchitis. She also took antibiotics and used an asthma inhaler due to the high humidity in Lima. Her mother shared her concerns with Alejandro, who waited for a break from school to take Toya to Pampas Grande.

Toya remembers, "My mother was crying when I left for Pampas Grande, thinking I would die from the elevation and the cold. Recently, when I went back to Pampas Grande for the first time in years, I realized just how much uncle Alejandro did for me. He took me and my first cousin Coty on horseback from Pariacoto. He tightly strapped us in, and we started what seemed like an endless journey. We went over mountain after mountain for hours. Fortunately, I couldn't see anything because it was dark. I could never have imagined the huge chasms we were crossing, and I was already scared enough from the dark, the loneliness, and the wilderness. We both wanted to cry, but uncle Alejandro was smart and witty, so he told us story after story that he had memorized.

We were little girls, so that was enough for us to calm down and enjoy the trip, and we arrived safe and sound at Quillcán. Fortunata was very attentive, welcoming us hospitably. She served us the typical local foods every day: fresh milk, cheeses, and potatoes as well as stews made in clay pots. In Quillcán, I played barefoot in the mud and in the torrential rain. I played with dirt and other things in nature. It was so different than life in Lima where everything was neat, clean, well-kept, and boiled and disinfected. If mom had known what Quillcán was like, she would have died! I spent those three months there then went back to Lima—completely allergy-free until this very day."

Toya gained weight in a few months and started dancing incredibly well—even being featured on the show "Peru Sings and Dances[11]" and representing Peru with her dance team in Mexico.

THE LEADER BREAKS NEW GROUND

Don Alejandro was also the first citizen of Pampas Grande to use banks. Just as planned, he mortgaged his farms to the bank and got his first loan from the Agrarian Bank of Peru. He wisely used the loan to rent the Acray estate for ten years from the Pampas Grande municipality. It was more than 250 acres located near the district's coast, and he bred goats there since they reproduce quickly.

Even though it was sandy, Acray had an unexplored river with great profit potential. He teamed up with his cheerful, blue-eyed friend from Cajamarca, Justino Sanchez Montoya. It was easy to get lost there, and both had to carry guns to protect themselves from the wild animals. They also had to suffer high temperatures, cactus thorns, and loneliness. Years later, however, Alejandro's older brother Gregorio would join them

---

11   "Perú Canta y Baila"

and they would rapidly grow their flock of goats. They discovered the potential of extracting vegetable wool, which was in demand as mattress stuffing, as well as vegetable charcoal, which is good for fuel, which they would transport to Huarmey to sell. He made a huge profit on both products as well as with broad breasted turkeys. Don Alejandro knew how to take advantage of Acray's perfect climate for raising turkeys.

THE RICH MAN'S GOATS

His son David, now a Siemens manager in Germany, remembers the following happening about that time:

"When I was playing in the plains at Quillcán, I saw a man pass with some goats. I wanted some, so I asked my father to buy me two of the kids. I cried until he caved—he always said, "You've got to indulge your children." Over time, those goats multiplied, covered the Coto mountain, and eventually reached Acray. A while later, I, already studying at the National University of Engineering, won a scholarship from INABEC to study in Germany. With the money I earned selling those goats—now more than 400 of them—I went to make a better future for myself."

Yoshio Ishisaka, the former vice president of Toyota Motor Corporation, says that all leaders must keep an open mind and love to travel. Don Alejandro had that, traveling constantly in his own country and others well into his old age.

AN UNWAVERING WORKER

Don Alejandro stayed in Acray for four or five hours and found wild donkeys and colts, which he brought to Quillcán to tame and use as pack animals. From that day on, he rode on horseback and became a skilled rider and tamer of wild horses. He was also very brave—he must have been, because he ate a hot rocoto pepper almost every day and drank the colostrum of his cows' milk.

The rich man's goats.

During that period of economic prosperity, he regularly traveled between Lima and Pampas Grande to supervise his businesses and spend time with his family, normally taking one of two routes to get from Pampas Grande to Lima. The first went through San Juan, Pashicuta, Pariaco-

Don Alejandro visiting the US.

to, and Huarmey. The second went through San Juan, Acray, El Molino, and Huarmey.

He supervised his store in Pampas Grande, lived with his family in San Juan to sow and reap the fields, looked after his pigs in Pashicuta, cared for his flock of goats in Acray, and worked as a contract bricklayer in Lima. The profits from each business were invested into building a proper house in Pampas, a farmhouse in Quillcán, and a house in Lima.

His cousin Manuel Castillo Ardiles reminisced, "500 years will pass before anyone like Alicho will come around again. He was a hard worker and generous—he would give you any animal you wanted and never said no to helping anyone, which is why God blessed him like Job. I saw how his animals multiplied in Acray."

"It is more blessed to give than to receive."
—Acts 20:35

In the background is his Quillcán house.

HONESTY WAS HIS GREATEST FORTUNE

One time, the Agrarian Bank gave don Alejandro an extra 10,000 soles with a loan. When he got home and counted the money, he realized the error—counting and recounting the money with his kids to make sure he wasn't mistaken. Sure enough, there was an extra 10,000 soles, so he immediately went back to the bank to return the extra money. The bankers were surprised to see him, but after doing a detailed cash count, they told him, "Don Alicho, if only there were ten Peruvians as honest as you, this would be a different country!"

He always acted with integrity and honesty—the two pillars of every great company in the world.

> "A good name is to be chosen rather than great riches,
> and favor is better than silver or gold."
> —Proverbs 22:1

ROCK SOLID CHARACTER

Around that time, he became a valued client and very important individual at the Agrarian Bank of Peru. He paid on time, had a solid constitution, and was respected wherever he went.

One day, he went to the Agrarian Bank to take out a loan, and they told him to come back the next week.

The next week, he came back like they had said, but they told him again to come back the next week.

He lost his patience and said loudly, "Who do you think I am? Some kind of idler like you all to have time to come back every week? I'm a working man, and I need that money to sow my fields! Don't you realize your success comes from hardworking clients like me? I want to talk with your boss!"

The boss came out looking embarrassed and immediately gave him the loan. After that, don Alejandro was treated well and they never made him wait in line.

> "Men are poor because they desire.
> I've been the poorest man in the world, but with faith in God,
> honesty, and hard work, I've been able to flourish."
> —A.A.C

HE WAS HARDWORKING AND PERSEVERING

Hugo Aguilar Ardiles, the president of the Peru-New Jersey Ancash Association in the United States remembers the following example of Alejandro's fortitude:

He grew many different varieties of potatoes in large quantities.

"A few years back, El Niño was severely affecting northern Peru, and Pampas Grande was cut off for two months by mudslides. It was raining horrendously, and my cousins and I, worried about our parents, went from Huarmey to Pampas. We were all surprised when we got to Quillcán and found uncle Alicho completely undisturbed. Even stranger, we was hilling up, fertilizing, and spraying his potato crop so they wouldn't rot from the extra rain.

"'In a case like this, potato blight is your worst enemy,' he said with the knowledge of a experienced farmer. All the good farmers knew about that, but they only sprayed twice at most, then they would give up in the incessant rains and relentless humidity. The only one dedicated enough to saving his crops to spray four times was uncle Alicho. As a result, he got the best potato harvest in the history of Pampas Grande. It was a clear example of his conviction and perseverance in everything he did. That was one of his greatest lessons for us."

A GREAT SPEAKER

They say that communication is the linchpin of being a great leader. He was particularly gifted, in that respect, to be a great speaker in both Quechua and Spanish. He could whip up crowds and inspire them with optimism and motivation. One particular instance, he gave a powerful speech to a group of young gas station pump attendants that burned itself onto each of their hearts and minds.

He said, "Boys, never let yourselves feel intimidated or inferior. Don't settle at your current job. Dream about owning a business like this one down the road. Everything depends on your willpower and hard work! Do your job well! Because to be a good boss, first you have to be a good employee!

Everyone around him noticed these traits of leadership and they respected him, which is how he easily found workers for everything he needed.

Family picnic, 1992.

Opening of Ardiles Hardware, 1982.

INTELLIGENT

One day, he had to leave the keys to his house in Quillcán for his son Alejandro. The problem was finding a place to hide them where he could find them since there was no method of communication to let him know. There was nobody trustworthy around with whom he could leave the keys, so he came up with a practical and clever idea. He left them above the window and stuck a trilingual sign on the door that said, "Llaves umachowindow," which means "The keys are above the window" in a mixture of Spanish, Quechua, and English. His son found them the next day and laughed thinking about his father's cleverness.

A DANCER

Don Alejandro dancing with his daughter Julia.

His niece Elena Valenzuela remembers, "Uncle Alejandro was an honest and excellent man in every way. He loved to tap dance, especially with me and his daughter Julia, whenever he took a break from his constant work."

He danced to everything with a contagious enthusiasm, and he said that you need three things to dance: a good floor, a good partner, and good music!

THE ORPHAN THAT INNOVATED HIS VILLAGE

Having decided to improve Quillcán, his ancestors' estate, he moved his family from the farmhouse in San Juan to Quillcán, where he had bought several farms.

"Kids, we're moving to Quillcán."

"But dad, the house there still isn't finished. Where are we going to live?" asked his children.

Don Alejandro, remembering that sometimes it's good for children to live with less, responded, "We're going to live in a log cabin. Only for a few days, God willing. Let's go!"

Marcela, his oldest daughter, remembers, "We had a log and straw cabin near a lloque tree. Dad made us a swing and hammock on the tree where we played from dawn till dusk—we were very happy. We ran around all day. One day, don Viterbo Maguiña visited us and told our mother, 'Just like their three meals, these kids should get three thrashings a day.' That scared us, but fortunately, our parents didn't pay him any attention. They hardly ever punished us."

It didn't take long before their brand-new house in Quillcán was finished. It was a dream house, with a gabled roof, red shingles, sturdy adobe walls, and a large yard where the Ardiles children and their cousins played day after day.

It was a wonderful time for Alejandro Ardiles. He had 5 children: Marcela, Ángel, Elena, Alejandro, and Julia. He and his wife played with their children, told them stories at dinner time, took them through the town at night on horseback, and taught them to work hard and to love and respect God above all.

"Daddy, who made the sun?" asked his son Bernabé one day.

"God!" he responded without hesitation.

"What about the moon?"

"God!"

"And the stars?"

"God as well!"

"He made all that? And he didn't get tired?"

"No! God never gets tired, son. He's omnipotent—he can do anything! He's omniscient—he knows everything! And he's omnipresent—he's everywhere!

"For his invisible attributes, namely, his eternal power and divine nature, have been clearly perceived, ever since the creation of the world, in the things that have been made."
—The Apostle Paul (Romans 1:20)

GROWING HIS TERRITORY

One day, he got up and noticed that his beloved Quillcán was large but unproductive. It boasted large but desolate fields and a horizon of hills full of thorn bushes and rocks.

He compared his ancestors' estate with the estates he had seen on the coast—full of cotton and sugarcane crops—and said, "The Ardileses were uli ricos [which means, "lying about being rich" in Quechua]. Why own property reaching the sea and only use a few parcels of it? This isn't even enough to eat! We're going to have to start from zero!"

That same day, he decided to turn all that unproductive land full of bushes and thorns into productive wheat, potato, and barley farms. He would sow on a large scale and sell the harvest not only in Huaraz, which was what the people in Pampas Grande normally did up until that point, but also in Lima. He planned to advance the farming professing, working vigorously from dawn till dusk to improve his economic situation and that of his hometown.

After making this decision, Alejandro prospered. He was the owner of his own business, an employer, and no longer a dime a dozen country worker in Lima—all thanks to his faith in God and the help and discernment of the Holy Spirit!

> "…and you shall go up and not down,
> if you obey the commandments of the LORD your God,
> which I command you today, being careful to do them."
> —Deuteronomy 28:13

04

HOW HE INNOVATED HIS VILLAGE

AAC's three rules for life.

To carry out his plan to sow on a large scale, don Alejandro determined three guidelines for his endeavor:

1. **Vision:** what did he hope to accomplish?

    Improve his children's futures, saving them from a cycle of poverty and mediocrity through education by having them study in the best schools and universities in Peru.

2. **Mission:** what strategies would he use to crystallize his vision?

    Turn his ancestor's estate into productive land by sowing on a large scale and becoming an excellent farmer.

3. **Values and principles:** he had deep faith in God and adopted the Incan ethics, "Ama llulla! Ama sua! Ama kella!", which means, "Don't steal! Don't lie! Don't be lazy!" He said them out loud and practiced them daily.

Unknowingly, he applied a Japanese principle: *imitate that which is good*. So, he applied all he had learned about farming and herding in Huarmey as well as the positive family atmosphere he learned from Emilio Servat, who was said to own half of Huarmey, who built a house in Lima, and who repeated the phrase "the best inheritance is an education" to his ten children. Don Alejandro imitated him, had ten children and built his own house in Lima near the University of Engineering. He imitated that which was good plus some.

His cousin Adolfo Fournier Ardiles, former Major of the Peruvian Army, recalls that, "Alejandro was exceptional. He was a careful observer, an early riser, a visionary, and he had a distinct personality that was always looking ahead. He set out to help Quillcán reach its full potential by sowing vast plots of land in the upper part (back then, there were the upper and lower parts). Quillcán was a vast estate stretching to the sea, so Alejandro had to fight with the Municipality of Huarmey over the borders. Nobody ventured out to those parts except him."

He was daring and brave. It was desolate, virgin land with unexplored ravines, wild valleys, and dangerous animals. He eventually acquired Acray, and his territory stretched to the edge of Huarmey.

VISION

A vision is imagining what you want in the future. Don Alejandro envisioned Quillcán as a prosperous estate with lush farms and various livestock, so he started to plan. What would he sow? He chose potatoes, wheat, and barley due to being in their natural habitat. With what capital? The capital would come from the Agrarian Bank's loans. With what personnel? He hired hands from far away in Huaraz, Chancos, Conchicos, and Marcará and worked to clear the rough land. With what tools? They used crowbars and pickaxes.

He risked large amounts of money on agriculture.

"Alicho was a hard worker!" emphasized his wife, doña Fortunata.

Once the land was cleared and arable, he fenced it, named it, and dedicated one plot to each of his children so that they would grow up with an owner's mentality.

"Daddy, whose is Tampush Pachan?"

"That's Marcela's—la Mama Vieja."

"Whose is Parihuanca?"

"Ángel's—Don Wuiño."

"Whose is La Corona?"

"Elenilla's—la Ponguilla[12]."

Unknowingly, he applied integral logistics and mastered supply chain management. He effectively managed resources from sowing to harvest, then transported the product to Pariacoto and Lima, the final point of sale.

---

12 La Mama Vieja, Don Wuiño, and la Ponguilla are nicknames

His son Bernabé relates that, "From early on, he exemplified hard work. He motivated his workers, encouraging them, joking with them, and patting them on the back. He also fed them, treated them well, paid fair wages, and only got angry when they were lazy, liars, or drunks."

Trips to Pariacoto carrying his harvest were like flying in an airplane—only God knew if there would be turbulence. Torrential rains with thunder and lightning appeared at the drop of a hat. The sky got dark, the rivers flooded, the bridges creaked, and there was no way to get to the other side. There was nobody to help in the middle of nowhere and nowhere to stay or buy food—they were difficult times.

This is the perfect example of how hard Alejandro worked, which is how he became a successful farmer!

A PIONEER IN WORKING WITH FERTILIZERS AND INSECTICIDES

His strategy to modernize his village consisted in bringing advanced technology from Peru's coast to the Andes. By introducing chemical fertilizers and new spraying techniques, he transformed agriculture in Pampas Grande. Using his own fertilization techniques, **he broke productivity records in the Cordillera Negra of the Andes!**

One time, agricultural engineers from the Agricultural University came to Pampas to teach the people to use agrochemicals effectively. They gave a community class and used percentages, but the farmers didn't understand anything about that. Alejandro wisely explained his

Hilling up don Alejandro's potato fields.

method of using empty tuna cans as a unit of measurement instead of percentages. All the farmers breathed a sigh of relief.

"Now we get it!" they exclaimed.

He made a bet with the engineers about the best way to fertilize.

"You plant in these two furrows and fertilize with your method. I'll plan in these two and use mine."

"No problem," they said.

Would you like to guess who harvested more potatoes? Alejandro won soundly.

His son Alex emphasizes, "There wouldn't be anything special about this humble farmer if he had used machines to sow and reap, roads to transport his supply and harvest, and advanced irrigation. The truth, however, is that he didn't have any of that. He did everything manually with hired hands, pack animals, and rain that God sent. **He set a great example for living well!**"

DON ALEJANDRO'S TIE-WEARING COWS

By that time, he had swine, goats, and turkeys, and the houses and farms of the next Ardiles generation began to slowly appear around Quillcán. Don Alejandro's "tie-wearing cows" lay in the pampas of Quillcán. They were distinct because they had a flap that looked like a tie. When they were calves, they cut a piece of the hide under their neck to claim them.

When he dabbled in bovine livestock, he was very successful. He worked hard year after year to become a successful herder, and he bought the best cows early in the morning to get the best bulls from the breeders in Pampas Grande and the neighboring areas.

AN EARLY RISER

His nephew Roman (17), now a US resident, remembers from that time, "One day, uncle Alicho and I had to get up at 3:30 A.M. to go about two and a half hours to Marnack where don Carlos Lirio, another well-known farmer, lived. Don Carlos normally left at 5:30. We got there just on time when he was leaving to sell livestock. We bought several young bulls and went back to Quillcán. We estimated their weights by looking at them—uncle Alicho was very good at estimating. We went around buying bulls from other breeders, always waking up early. He taught me to be honest, hardworking, and an early riser. We stumbled around in total darkness. Nothing scared him. He had a deep faith in God and always fought to keep moving forward!"

Ángel, his oldest son, who is now Chief Physician and Head of Nephrology at the Rebagliati Hospital in Lima, remembers a work day when his dad was starting out as a herder. "We were tired after working all day on the farm. We unyoked the oxen and took them to the spring to drink. After, they each stayed in their respective pens to eat and sleep. The next day, we had to work again, but that night, a young untamed bull from Quipash ran away in the dark. We chased it, but couldn't reach it. The downpour and the darkness kept me from seeing clearly, and there were thorns on the route, so I couldn't run in my old, broken shoes. The hired hands couldn't reach it either, so we were about to give up when my father got there in defiance of the night and the mud to capture the animal. We returned at dawn covered in mud and with thorns all in our feet, but with the animal. I learned that you should never give up no matter how many odds are against you."

With his knowledge of construction, Alejandro built troughs with water from the spring for the animals. They were strong and well-built, and it was pleasing to see the clear water from the springs.

His niece—the daughter of his sister Antonieta—Elena Valenzuela Ardiles, a psychologist, remembers, "He always treated his animals well, calling them by their names, giving them fresh water and food, and treating them with love like they were part of the family."

A GOOD APPRAISER

His son David comments, "When I think about my dad, I have a lot of emotional memories, especially of when I used to go with him on trips to transport cows from Pampas Grande to Lima for his livestock business.

"When I was 11 or 12, I started driving cattle with him to the slaughterhouse at Garagay. I remember a lot of stories from those trips—most of them enlightening—that changed my character and my life so much.

"I learned a lot from those difficult trips—from buying cows in Pampas and the surrounding towns to transporting them to Lima and overseeing the process of slaughtering them to selling the meat. From rounding up, herding, and fattening the cows to weighing and pricing each one. I even learned tricks to pass control points and get the cows into the slaughterhouse by using 'grease money.'"

> "Life isn't measured in achievement, not in years alone."
> —Bruce McLaren

IN CONTROL

Never having studied administration, he planned, managed, and controlled finances and produced and sold his products. He managed his business like the big businessmen, keeping an accounting book where he wrote all his livestock and agricultural operations. As soon as an animal was born, he wrote it down and assigned its ownership to one of his children. They were each responsible for caring for their animals, meaning he gave them responsibility as well as authority.

"Dad, what are we going to call this calf?" asked Alex.

"Call it Planta, son."

"Whose will it be?"

"Yours, papacito[13]," he said while laughing and lifting it in his strong arms.

HE TURNED CHALLENGES INTO OPPORTUNITIES FOR GROWTH

"Moooo!"

His tie-wearing cows mooed in front of his house at Quillcán because there was no grass or water for them. However, Don Alejandro turned challenges into growth opportunities. During droughts, he would take a horse to the coast to rent alfalfa fields in Huamba or Huarmey. Then he would move his cows there until the drought passed. While there, he took the opportunity to sell milk to pay for his flock's food.

As a herder, he worked with large quantities of money. Thank God he was smart and had pants made with double military pockets and got a permit to carry a pistol. He was brave, and nobody attacked him. He was a man of character.

Over the years, he bought his own vehicles to transport his animals and harvests, driving his own trucks and vans from Lima to Pampas Grande and back. His first car was a Hillman Hunter, and he later bought his first truck—a Dodge Santa Elena 300 WG-300. He called his trucks

---

13 A term of endearment, especially from parent to son. The female equivalent is "mamacita."

"Ñato Lindo" in honor of Christian Daniel, his grandson that he loved very much.

He learned to drive when he was 50, proving that anyone can learn at any age.

"Things will go well at the end for those who fear the Lord"
—Ecclesiasticus 1:13

Above: He transported his harvests in his truck. The majestic Canchón is visible in the background.

Right: With his dear grandson, Christian Daniel.

QUILLCÁN—HEAVEN ON EARTH

Over the years of hard work, Quillcán became a heaven on earth with its perfect climate, bright sun, blue skies, and clouds like snowflakes. It looked beautiful! The new fields full of wheat, potatoes, white and purple flowers, and golden ears of barley bobbed in the breeze. Don Alejandro's dream had come true! His property was covered with clovers and chard and the pattering feet of chickens, dogs, cats, pigs, donkeys, horses, cows, and sheep.

However, there were also very cloudy days. When the rainstorms came, lightning flashed and thunder boomed deafeningly, but the storms always passed just like our problems. The sky cleared, a rainbow appeared, and the sun shined once again on the flittering partridges and doves.

AN EXCELLENT HUNTER

The landscape was beautiful. Alejandro, followed by his sons Ángel and Alex, grabbed his shotgun and went into the mountains to hunt deer, viscachas, and partridges. Every time they spotted a target, they shot it. When they got home. doña Fortunata cooked delicious soups that they shared with their friends and family. Nobody ever attacked him because he always had a shotgun and carried a pistol. He was sure of himself and very brave.

UNFORGETTABLE NIGHTS IN QUILLCÁN

Soccer was don Alejandro's great passion and he infected those around him, starting with his children, family, and partners.

His oldest son Angel remembers, "Every day, we finished work exhausted and ate dinner early at about six or seven in the evening. While we finished up in the kitchen, dad would go into the living room and soon the entire Quillcán pampas was lit up by Petromax lanterns. He and our cousins were always the San Juan team, and the workers were always the Matará team. I remember the first jersey he bought me. It was a blue Sporting Cristal jersey. I wore in it night after night, which made him extremely happy."

His niece Violeta, the daughter of his sister Laura, now a resident of the US, recalls those times as well. "It wasn't just the men or even the adults who played soccer in Quillcán. We all played—cousins, uncles, aunts, owners, day laborers—night after night. Like children, we played tag, hide and seek, freeze tag, and tons of other games. My uncle Alejandro brought us all together!"

FIVE "HUACHACAZOS"

In the glowing evenings at Quillcán, before the sun set and after finishing his daily chores, Alejandro played cards with his kids, using old sacks as mats on the porch of his house and eating toasted wheat with cheese.

He was such a good player against his friends that they said, "Instead of playing against him, I'll just give him my wallet."

With his kids, he played without money so they wouldn't fall into the vice of gambling, but he never let them win on purpose because he wanted to teach them the there are winners and losers in life. It also taught them to have a good memory and keep mental accounts, which might be why seven of his kids became engineers.

He called the rounds of cards "huachacazos," which is the Quechua word for "lashings."

One night, years later when they lived in Lima, he started playing with his sons. His daughter Julia had gone to bed early that night because she had a college test the next day, but the laughing and joking between the father and sons while playing cards kept her from sleeping. It was already midnight when she heard her father say, "OK, just five more huachacazos."

Julia got up and said, "Five huachacazos? When are you going to let me sleep?"

Don Alejandro loved his kids very much, so he ended the game immediately.

"Taking life with a good sense of humor is a foolproof recipe for happiness."
—Anonymous

AN OUTSTANDING MAN

Don Alejandro was very intelligent. When he traveled from Pampas Grande to Lima, he carried a large quantity of cheese that doña Fortunata had prepared after milking his cows. He also brought bags of potatoes, wheat, and barley to share with friends and family and to sell. On the way, he stopped at his friend Jhovani Terlevich's house at the El Molino hacienda near Huarmey. Jhovani was a very proper and happy Yugoslavian man who ran the hacienda. Alejandro shared his harvests with him and received hospitality and aid in return. He also stopped by his dear friend Quirino Malgarejo's house in Huarmey.

He never went anywhere with empty hands. He was very generous. Upon returning to Pampas Grande from Lima, he brought boxes of cakes, candy, and cookies as well as dozens of preserves and bags of fruits to share with kids and adults. Everyone loved him very much.

A neighbor of Pampas Grande remembers those times. "If uncle Alicho came, he came with the Lord's blessing."

> "Serrano, if only there were ten Peruvians like you, this would be a different country."
> —Jhovani Terlevich

POTATOES WITH VITAMINS A TO Z

His daughter Edith, a petroleum engineer, says that "The difference between my dad and the other villagers in Pampas was that he sowed and worked hard with faith in God that it would rain. The others crossed their arms, looked at the sky, and said, 'No rain this year. It'll be a bad year.'

"Dad, on the other hand, worked so hard that I think God took compassion on him and sent rain to water his crops. I've never seen so much money in my whole life. In 1984, I went with him to the harvest, and he pulled up potatoes by the truckload. When he sold them, they paid him so much money that they carried it in sacks."

There's a story about a pessimistic shoe salesman who went to Africa. A short while later, he sent a telegram saying, "I'm coming back—nobody wears shoes here." On the other hand, an optimistic shoe salesman wrote back, "Send more shoes—everyone here needs them."

Everything in this life depends on attitude. Don Alejandro knew that nobody in the Peruvian jungle ate potatoes, so he went into the Amazon forest to sell them. He carried them by the ton in trucks. He and his son David went through the cities making sales pitches with a catchy slogan: "Potatoes! Potatoes! Potatoes with vitamins A to Z!" The people laughed and bought them.

Alejandro also cleverly sold his barley crop in the Monterrico Hippodrome in Lima where they raced thoroughbred horses, and he made a nice profit. He became the best farmer Pampas Grande had ever seen.

His cousin Manuel Castillo Ardiles says, "Alejandro was incredibly capable of making money in rugged places like Pampas—at more than 11,000 feet of altitude, full of thorns, steep hills, far from rivers, and with just a few creeks. He used only the rains to water his crops, and there was no advanced technology or highway."

He made money in the middle of nowhere because he believed that "All hard work pays off and your will is your only limit."

That is how he became the best farmer of all time in Pampas and received a position as president of the Ancash Agrarian Directors Association, which covered four districts: Pira, Cajamarquilla, Huanchay, and Pampas Grande. He enthusiastically met the responsibilities of the position, supporting breeders and farmers so that they could produce more and receive loans from the Agrarian Bank.

Don Alejandro also petitioned the Congress of Peru to establish a law allowing bricklayers to receive proper housing. He thought it unjust that bricklayers built houses, mansions, and buildings but had no place to live. He also made a petition for a law that would mandate fair prices for food products sold by farmers, since they provided for the most basic of human needs.

> "A wise man is full of strength,
> and a man of knowledge enhances his might."
> —Proverbs 24:5

05
HE SERVED IN POLITICS WITHOUT PAY

Many believe that only idle people are interested in politics. In reality, the opposite is true. Let's rise to John F. Kennedy's challenge. "Ask not what your country can do for you—ask what you can do for your country."

GOVERNOR OF PAMPAS

When Pampas Grande elected him as governor (a representative of the President of Peru) in 1954, don Alejandro, at the age of 36, already exhibited incredible social leadership with his trustworthiness, eloquence, and motivating power. Back then, leaders were not compensated; rather, they often had to utilize their own wealth to fulfill the duties of the position.

Alejandro paid out of pocket to execute public works, giving up his free time, overcoming many difficulties, and sacrificing his interests and desires. As all politicians should act in an ideal world, he served generously and never sought personal gain.

Among his most important accomplishments of that time are the following:

- He considered education and sports to be essential for children, so he created and managed a proposal to create the first high school in all of the Cordillera Negra with the slogan, "Education is the best weapon against backwardness and poverty."

- He organized the first area soccer championship in Pampas, with teams from La Victoria, Shancac, Matara, Chorrillos, and San Juan. Don Alejandro's homeland, San Juan, won.

- He also organized the first regional soccer championship of the west side of the Andean Cordillera Negra, with teams from the districts of Pira, Cajamarquilla, Huanchay, and Pampas Grande.

DON ALICHO AT CITY HALL

Being a man of faith, integrity, and hard work, Alejandro was elected mayor of Pampas Grande for two consecutive terms: 1961-1962 and 1963-1964. His excellent leadership was recognized not only by the local population, but also by the authorities of the neighboring districts and Huaraz, the capital of the Ancash region, due to his honesty and efficiency.

Even though it was extremely difficult to gain provincial prestige back then—the trip from Pampas Grande to Huaraz taking at least two days on horseback—Alejandro stuck out among the local authorities.

Plaza de Armas of Pampas Grande before Alejandro Ardiles became mayor.

> "His master said to him, 'Well done, good and faithful servant. You have been faithful over a little; I will set you over much.'"
> —Matthew 25:23

HIS MASTERPIECE

Alejandro accomplished many things, but his masterpiece was undoubtedly the design, construction, and management of the first high school in Pampas Grande—now called the National School of San Jerónimo—in 1964. To accomplish this, he made countless presentations before the Peruvian Congress, the Ministry of Education in Lima, and the Government Palace. Thanks to the help of his friend Saturnino Berrospi Méndez, an APRA[14] deputy, he interviewed with former Peruvian President Fernando Belaúnde Terry.

Manuel Castillo Ardiles, Alejandro's cousin, remembers the encounter. "Bathed and well dressed, eight Ardiles first cousins went to the Government Palace. Among them were Alejandro, Augusto, Guillermo,

Opening of the first high school in the Cordillera Negra of the Andes: "San Jerónimo," Pampas Grande, 1963.

---

14   American Popular Revolutionary Alliance

Juan, Julio, and myself, as well as Alejandro's 5-year-old son Bernabé to represent the youth of Pampas Grande."

His son Alex emphasizes, "The construction of what is now the National School of San Jerónimo wouldn't be so important if you didn't realize that Municipalities didn't have the budget to undertake projects of this magnitude back then. My father's leadership and skill in organizing the project and engaging each household were the enabling factors for this great project."

He gathered the Pampas Grande community to tell them, "We are going to lay the first stone of the high school." Everyone thought they were going to dance and eat free food since Alejandro had slaughtered his bull and hired a band. Instead, they heard a speech in both Quechua and Spanish motivating them to organize and work together. He then treated the volunteers to a feast. Each household was to build a classroom, and he promised a prize to the one that finished first. According to his nephew Roman, he offered one thousand soles from his own pocket to the winners—a sum equaling around $10,000 USD today—thereby encouraging healthy competition between the households.

Later, he personally donated books, furniture, and tools to the National School of San Jerónimo, which began operations in 1965 under the oversight of professor Hernán Arguedas Loli. He hoped that the school would serve as an example to the neighboring districts.

Don Alejandro was convinced that the best route to progress is education, which is why he encouraged students to study more by implementing two prizes with funds from his own pocket:

- **The "Golden Pencil" Prize,** which gave a pen with the engraved name of the first-place winner each year.

- **The Cash Prize** for former students who studied at the best universities in the country like the National University of San Marcos, the National University of Engineering, and the National Agrarian University.

> "Leaders think and act first, and they feel later."
> —Anonymous

HE PROMOTED SPORTS IN PAMPAS

He was a sports icon in Pampas according to his first cousin Manuel Castillo Ardiles:

"Alejandro played several sports, and he always wanted to be the best. He had already played every sport in Pampas—he seemed invincible. I'm not exaggerating. I would even dare say that his ten children together aren't as good as he was. During the National Holidays in Pampas Grande, there were various organized sports and everyone participated, but Alejandro competed in every single one. He was the best in foot races, high jump, and long jump. Even though he was only medium height, his team always won. One day, a tall boxing champion named Jerónimo, also from Pampas and in the Peruvian Navy, came and challenged Alejandro to a boxing match. Alejandro was tired from competing all day, but he accepted. He was shorter, but quicker and rascally. In the blink of an eye, Jerónimo was lying on the ground. The punch was so strong that people had to help him to his feet. His stamina was such that he woke up early the next morning while everyone else was still sleeping to tend to the farm, carrying corn stalks and food for his animals. Alejandro worked hard, ate well, and played sports because he believed that 'idleness is the mother of all vice.'"

He founded the "Pampas Grande Sports Union" (UDP) in Lima mainly for his cousins. Later, the club was moved to Pampas Grande, where it served as an example for the organization of other sports clubs. He organized regional championships and encouraged sports among children, adolescents, and young adults by giving them balls, uniforms, and cleats.

Hugo Aguilar, his nephew, recalls, "My uncle Alejandro was the heart and soul of UDP, whose rivals were CDP, the Social Center, and Sport Progreso."

These soccer teams mark the golden age of inter-club sports in our village, while San Juan (the team he loved and the only one to play in the department final of the Peru Cup in Huaraz in the 70s), Chorrillos, Shancac, and Matará—the eternal "shadow of San Juan"—shined in the area competitions.

> "Give, and it will be given to you."
> —Luke 6:38

06

A RIGOROUS SPIRITUAL LIFE AND A HAPPY, UNITED FAMILY

When I was a girl, I saw my father plow lands that had never been tilled. The first time through, large rocks kept appearing and he would haul them out. The next time, the rocks were smaller, and he threw them to the sides. This process went on and on to break through the land. It took many trips through before the land was well plowed.

When we surrender our lives to God, a similar process starts. At first, there might be large sins, but the word of the Lord penetrates to our soul and sheds light on other sins so that we can throw them out and be cleansed.

It's important to understand that all humans are body, soul, and spirit. The body is the visible and tangible; the soul consists of thoughts, feelings, and emotions; and the spirit connects with God.

Normally, we eat three meals a day. We also feed our souls by studying and gaining knowledge about life. However, we neglect our spirit not knowing that the **most important decision a human can make is surrendering his life to God,** which ensures both eternal life in heaven and abundant life on earth!

Don Alejandro gave his life up to God because of one bright evening in 1965 in Quillcán. He was inoculating his cows from different deadly diseases like anthrax, foot-and-mouth disease, tuberculosis, and mastitis when he unknowingly touched his right eyelid with the cotton that was coated with the vaccine. The next day, when he woke up with a swollen eye, he was concerned and went to find a doctor in the village.

"It was the only time I ever led the horse my father was riding. I wanted to talk, but he was quieter than ever—he hardly even said, 'yes,' 'no,' or 'maybe.' He never showed how worried he was. I only understood later how serious the situation was."

His good friend Don Justino Sanchez gave him first aid, but his sister Laura had him transported on a litter to Pariacoto and later by bus to Lima due to the severity. The infection had worsened so quickly that by the time he got to Lima he looked like a two-headed monster. Thankfully, he was admitted to the Maison de Santé clinic where they miraculously saved him.

His brother-in-law Porfirio Valenzuela, who was with him, said, "I didn't sleep at all the first night Alicho was in the hospital because the doctors said the infection was moving quickly toward his brain, meaning the chance of survival was low. They told me to prepare for the worst. He already had eight young kids."

His brother-in-law Porfirio Valenzuela, his wife doña Fortunata, his nephew Edgardo Fiorito, his sister Antonieta, and his brother Gregorio.

Lying at the death's door, don Alejandro felt his world was crumbling around him. Feverish and lacking the strength even to talk, he thought he would die soon. Then, he remembered don Demetrio Támara and doña Dionisia, Christians that had talked to him about God's infinite power—his healing when men recognize their sin, repent, and give their lives to God. He remembered that God would give all the desires of a man's heart to him if he followed those steps.

Then, he accepted God and received him into his heart with faith. He took God as his heavenly doctor with the conviction that "When man no longer can, God begins to act."

> "For nothing will be impossible with God."
> —Luke 1:37

Miraculously, he recovered so quickly that he even escaped from the clinic in his pijamas one evening to see Pelé, the King of Soccer, in the National Stadium.

He was later baptized in the Pucaquita pond in Pampas. As tribute to his miracle, he donated a piano to the Pampas Grande Evangelical Church to praise God through music. He sent it through the missionary Walter Erickson. From then on, his priorities changed radically—first God, then family, then work.

> "All things are possible for one who believes."
> —Mark 9:23b

HIS WIFE—HIS IDEAL HELPER

The second most important decision a human can make is choosing a good partner. Don Alejandro wisely chose Fortunata, who closely matched the description of the virtuous woman in Proverbs 31. She was a hard worker, a servant, and she cared for her children, nieces, nephews, and anyone else who came to her houses in Pampas or Lima. She served the needy, kept her gardens, sewed double quilts for her kids, and took care of her servants.

Her nephew Reynaldo Trinidad, a well-known Peruvian journalist and founding director of the *Agronoticias*[15] review, remembers her well. "It seems liked my aunt Fortu's pots were bottomless. She served everyone who came to her house."

Her daughter Elena says, "I saw my mother up close. She was a virtuous woman with a flirtatious husband. He always flirted with girls, but instead of trying to change him or making him an object of jealousy, she rooted her feet in God. She prayed for him, and God kept her sane and healthy and gave her a stable home. Because of my mother's prayers, God saved my father from many evils and dangerous women.

Doña Fortunata testifies, "I stayed in Quillcán to take care of our kids, animals, and crops when Alejandro went to Lima. My daily routine started by going to the Huiyó spring to get barrels of water with the donkeys because I couldn't carry them myself. I put them on the donkeys to carry them back to the house. Thankfully, Alejandro was smart and cautious, caring not only for himself but also for all of us. He brought back calamine cylinders and sheets which he used to make gutters just under the edge of the roof so that we could use the water runoff that got stored

---

15 A combination between the words meaning "Agriculture" and "News"

in the cylinders. That water was very useful. When we needed to wash clothes, we went to Huiyó.

"I also bathed the kids there and took the opportunity to correct them. When they were naked, I would smack their butts and sternly ask, "Pichucunquiraccu?" which means "Are you going to go get dirty again?" in Quechua. When Alicho bathed our kids, he played, jumped, splashed, and laughed with them, which is why they didn't want to take baths with me. He loved them so much."

Don Alejandro with his wife Fortunate and his son Alex.

Both were faithful to God, and their lives reflected that. Christ was the head of the house. They prayed often (especially before meals and in the mornings and evenings), and they worshipped and had devotionals in their house, which is why they and their ten children enjoyed a happy, unified household.

EDUCATION—THE BEST INHERITANCE

Don Alejandro knew that it was not diamonds or oil that made a country rich—it was education and manners. Education and manners mean that when you can rob, you don't; that when someone is walking on the street and the sidewalk is narrow, you let them on and say "Excuse me;" and that you give a fair wage when getting a product or service. Education is the vehicle for the development of all people and all nations, which is why Alejandro never spared any expense or effort on his children's education.

Marcela, his oldest daughter, won a scholarship to study in Huaraz in 1960 after graduating top of her class in the Pampas Primary School. She happily showed the scholarship to her dad, who said, "No, sweetheart, you're not going to study in Huaraz--you could marry any old drunk there. I'm taking you to Lima."

Alejandro had bigger goals for her and her siblings—to take them to Lima to study in the best schools and universities in the capital. He bought two side-by-side lots in the engineering district[16] and built a house near the University of Engineering. It is no coincidence that seven of his ten children are now engineers.

They originally traveled with his niece Coty, his sister Laura's daughter. In Lima, they stayed in Breña in his sister Antonieta's and her husband Porfirio Valenzuela's house. Years later, they moved into their own

---

16 A region of Lima called Urbanización Ingeniería

house and Marcela graduated top of her class and received an advanced diploma from Elvira García y García high school in Pueblo Libre, Lima. In doing so, she honored her parents' sacrifices and set an example for her younger siblings, who would go on finishing their studies every two years.

HOW HE TIGHTLY UNITED HIS FAMILY

Alejandro always told his kids, "There are ten of you, but to me, you're all one. If you have something, share it." He united his family in love for God and sports, also organizing weekly family walks. He sacrificed his time and even carried the daughters that couldn't keep up with the ten. During the summers, they went to the northern or southern beaches.

Back then, the beautiful Santa Rosa beach was exclusively for soldiers, but they were able to go there thanks to their oldest son Ángel, who was a military doctor. They would go in two cars, packed in like happy

FC Ardiles. Standing: Ángel, César, AAC, and Carlos. Kneeling: Alex, David, Bernabé, and his grandson Pedro David as the newest player.

Family picnic.

sardines with their own lunches and soups in huge pots that they ate after praying in a circle. After a short nap, they played soccer and had volleyball, basketball, and swimming tournaments while the smallest kids made sand castles. They were wonderful evenings.

During the winters, they went to El Naranjal park for more than ten years in a row. They held competitions where Alejandro was either a player or the self-proclaimed "very partial referee." Alex and his five brothers—Ángel, Alex, Bernabé, David, César, and Carlos—formed a soccer team that they called "FC Ardiles." Their dad was the coach, and they went into every game ready to win.

As time went on and the children began to work, the economic situation of the family improved. They stopped bringing all their own food and started going to the telephone company Cervatel's recreation center where Bernabé was a junior manager. The Ardiles family was known for being unified. Alejandro's sons invited rival teams to play against FC Ardiles. They took the games seriously and won at all costs.

The most athletic of the family were his daughter Edith, who was an excellent basketball player and a boxer capable of beating any other person of her age—some of whom are now soldiers—and Carlos, who was such a good striker that people said he played like Maradona.

His oldest son Ángel also got his father's passion for soccer—so much so that he came to be part of the San Marcos University San Fernando College of Medicine soccer team.

Ángel remembers, "One Saturday morning, I told dad and my brothers, 'I'm going to play against Alianza Lima today in Matute Stadium.' They thought I was kidding, so I gave them the address and left. When I entered the stadium with the San Fernando team, I saw my dad proudly sitting in the stands with some of my brothers. I was captain that morning against Alianza Lima. I had long since learned his lessons about playing and winning."

The quality time he spent with his family lead him to stay healthy. Being mentally and physically healthy is a requirement for being a successful individual, and everyone has seen how small problems can affect output at work. It's important to maintain balance in life and control eating, sleeping, exercising, and recreation habits to keep our bodies and minds in shape.

Everyone knows it's important to be sociable and interact with others, but it's also good to go to sleep early to maintain a good schedule.

PERU, THE CHAMPION!

When Peru qualified for the World Cup in 1970 and 1978, he watched the games with his entire family—so focused that you could have stolen everything from around him. He didn't want anyone to bother him. The atmosphere was festive, joyful, and tense. Those were the glory days of Peruvian soccer, and people chanted, "Peru, the champion!" in the streets.

Being in Alejandro's Lima house with him was like being at the actual World Cup. The same thing happened when the Peruvian volleyball team played. His sons did not want any girls to see the games, saying, "Dad, don't let the girls watch because they're going to mess our team up!"

Don Alicho smiled and said, "Be quiet! That's not true. My girls have to watch!" He made no distinction between sexes.

When Peru won, he took all his kids and neighbors around in his truck to shout, "Peru! Peru! Peru!" and sing the popular song, "Peru, the champion[17]!"

He even taught all his children—male and female—how to box so that they would be able to defend themselves. Traditionally, "to be an Ardiles" means to love God, studies, sports, and work. His greatest legacy was leaving happy and unified kids.

> "Behold, how good and pleasant it is
> when brothers dwell in unity!"
> —Psalm 133:1

---

[17] "Perú, Campeón" by Los Ases del Perú

07
ON BEING A GOOD FATHER

A sheltered and spoiled child develops a self-entitled attitude, always puts himself first, and never recognizes the effort his parents put into him. When we're the type of parent that shelters, are we loving are kids or ruining them? You can give your kids a big house, good food, piano lessons, and a big screen TV, but also give them the experience of cutting the grass. After eating, let them wash the dishes together—not because you don't have the money to hire someone to do it, but because you want to love them well. No matter how rich you are, one day your hair will turn gray, and what's important is that your kids understand to appreciate other people's work, to live through difficulty, and to learn how to do good work in a team.

It's important that your children learn to recognize and appreciate other people's suffering, that they do not become the type of person whose only goal is money, and that they learn to appreciate the value of family and community. By showing both love and firmness to his kids and applying the following lessons, don Alejandro accomplished just that.

TOUGH LOVE

He instilled a love for studies and for work in them. When his kids were in school in Lima, if one of them didn't want to do their homework, he didn't get on to them. He just said, "If you don't want to study, let's go herd pigs and goats in Acray!" He said it with such finality that each child quietly got to work.

He also gave them responsibility. In 1969, taking advantage of their strategic location in the Engineering District in Lima, he opened little businesses that the children ran while he kept working in Pampas as a farmer and herder. First, he opened a jugería[18], then a bodega[19], then a butcher shop. In doing so, he showed them how much work it takes to be successful.

César, his ninth child, now a well-known ironmonger, says, "I remember when dad would get to the Lima house early in the morning with a truckload of cows. He would wake us up and tell us to go with him to feed the animals. I told myself, 'Man, my dad is terrible! Why right now at 3 AM?' Now, I'm forever thankful because I know that hard work is the only way to go far in life. I clearly remember helping slaughter the animals in the shop. Dad showed me how to avoid ruining parts of the meat with the machines. I was still a kid (14) and I was scared to see the blood, but there it was. He would have me count the money we made selling the meat, which was about $10,000. When I finished, he asked, 'Did you count well, don Shesha?' and I said, 'Yes sir, it's right,' and he never recounted the money. He always inspired self-confidence and—without me realizing it—he was already preparing me to be a businessman."

> "Whoever spares the rod hates his son,
> but he who loves him is diligent to discipline him."
> —Proverbs 13:24

---

18 A type of juice store common in Peru that sells fresh squeezed juices
19 A small grocery store similar to American drug stores or corner stores

A PRESENT FATHER MAKES EXCELLENT STUDENTS

Most parents in Pampas enrolled their students in April, got their report cards in December, and then spanked their kids in their houses for getting bad grades. On the other hand, don Alejandro constantly supervised his children's studies and even visited their classrooms to have dialogues like the following:

"So, professor Cochachín, let's do an evaluation of my oldest son Ángel to see how much he's learning."

"Very well, don Alicho. I'll ask him about the lesson. Angelito, do cows say moo?"

"Yes sir."

"Angelito, do roosters have beaks and say 'cock-a-doodle-doo?'"

"Yes sir."

"Very good! You get an A plus!"

Alejandro called attention to this type of teacher with no imagination or pedagogical skill, but he publicly also praised primary school teachers and encouraged parents to visit their kids' schools to lift their spirits.

As a result of this interest in his children's schooling, all of them became professionals.

HE PROTECTED HIS CHILDREN'S SELF-ESTEEM

One morning, Alejandro went to his daughter Elena's classroom and her teacher told her, "Show your father what you have in your pockets."

Elena took out some jacks, and the teacher harshly said, "Look, don Alicho, your daughter always has her jacks! I'm going to take them away."

Alejandro responded, "Why would you do that? Toys are a treasure for kids."

The teacher looked embarrassed. Alejandro didn't make fun of his daughter; instead, he supported her. Years later, Elena graduated with a social work degree from the University of San Martín de Porres, completed her master's in Social Programs at the National University of San Marcos, and works at an international NGO called World Vision.

His son David remembers, "One thing I'll never forget is how loving my father was. When I was four or five years old, I came up to him when he was meeting with some authorities in the Pampas Grande Plaza. Without hesitation, he picked me up. I was eating a banana and my hands were covered in it. Dad was going to a public event and I dropped a piece of banana on his white shirt. I instinctively tried to clean it off, but just made it worse with my hands. To my surprise, instead of getting frustrated, he laughed and went on at the event like nothing had happened. That assured me of his love for me, and I'll always be deeply grateful to him for that."

68-year-old Alejandro at his son David's goodbye party in 1986.

HE LOVED AND PROTECTED HIS CHILDREN

Every time he came back home, it was a party for the kids. He came with a heart full of love and saddlebags full of breads, rice, cakes, fruits, and other foods. The kids could sense it when he was coming back. When they heard the clap of the hooves in the distance, they all looked at the road trying to make out his silhouette. The moment they glimpsed it, they ran like little chicks to meet him.

"Daddy! Daddy!" They ran with outstretched arms, wanting to touch him before he could hop off the horse. He pulled the smallest ones up into his lap.

When he dismounted, he hugged and kissed everyone and sang each child's song, lifting them up and dancing with them. It really was a party! He made each feel like king or queen of the world with the healthy and happy environment he provided. They drank fresh milk from their cows, then ate fresh cheese with freshly harvested potatoes. They rode donkeys and horses next to their father.

HE MOTIVATED HIS CHILDREN

From the time they were little, he always encouraged his children to "think big." When Fortunata told them, "Work hard, even if you're trash men," don Alejandro would shoot back, "How can you say that? They're going to be doctors and engineers!"

He called his sons with the honorifics "Don" or "Papacito." For example, he would say "don Bernabé," "don Wiño," "don Shesha," and so on. In doing so, he motivated them and made them feel special.

One clear success of this was in 1956, when his fourth child Alejandro (or Alex) was barely two years old. Don Alejandro would say to him, "Ah, Nuna! You brave Peruvian engineer! You only win by fighting!" He called him that into his old age.

He called him "engineer" without having any idea how competitive the National University of Engineering would be or how difficult it is to study petroleum engineering. However, as time passed, his premonition came true. Alex worked for more than 25 years and became Senior Manager at the multinational Occidental Petroleum Corporation (OXY).

WHAT HE DID WHEN HIS CHILDREN GOT BAD GRADES

"Never discourage a student. If she gets a bad grade, don't punish her. Encourage her by telling her that life has ups and downs."
—Alejandro Ardiles Caja

In Alejandro's day, "knowledge is won with blood" was a well repeated saying that he never followed. Back then, if a student misbehaved, the teacher punished him with a three-stranded whip.

His daughter Julia says, "I remember the day I got my first term's report card like it was yesterday. When my teacher gave it to me, she drew her thumb across her throat. When the bell rang at the end of the day, dad came to get me on his red horse, "Galanteo," who had a white forehead and white feet. Dad was still young with honey-colored eyes and dark brown hair. He looked handsome.

"I innocently and enthusiastically said, 'Dad, look! I got my report card, but for some reason my teacher did like this,' and I drew my finger across my throat.

"Dad laughed and said, 'Ha ha ha, Julia Josefina! Don't pay her any attention. Let's go,' and he pulled me up before we galloped away.

That would have been so different with other parents! When their kids got bad grades, they called them 'Stupid!' or asked, 'Why didn't you study?' Dad never did anything of the sort, and that was one of his greatest lessons."

HE PRAISED HIS CHILDREN'S ACCOMPLISHMENTS

When his children got good grades, won medals, diplomas, etc., he celebrated with them. One of the momentous occasions in the family was in 1970 when Alex got accepted into the university—it had been one of his biggest dreams since 1956.

Another was when David (19), after taking five national exams went to Germany in 1982 with a full scholarship. He was competing with students from trilingual schools (English, Spanish, and German), whereas he had only studied in the GUE Ricardo Bentin del Rimac school and was in college. That was news that even spread over radio shows in Peru: "The son of a farmer is traveling to Germany to study electrical engineering with a full scholarship."

He got to see many of his children's successes during his life. His son Bernabé went to college first place in his field, which was also announced in large newspapers.

Each time he celebrated, he invited his close relatives over for a feast and gave a speech saying that everything came from God. He also celebrated his kids' birthdays. It's scientifically proven that this improves a person's self-esteem.

His daughter Edith recalls, "One January 17th, we celebrated my and my brother David's birthdays in the pampas at Quillcán. That morning, the sound of burning stalks of dry wheat and barley woke me up while they were burning the bristles off a recently slaughtered hog. All of the kids—curious, surprised, and exhilarated at the same time—watched while the fire burned the bristles off. Later, they skinned the pig and prepared a large lunch for family and friends in Quillcán. Every February 2nd, cooks

August 3, 1982: David leaving for Germany with a full scholarship.

paraded around peeling guinea pigs and slicing hams to celebrate the birthday of their son Alejandro--the "engineer" and their "Nuna."

HUG EACH OTHER! KISS EACH OTHER!

When kids fight, most parents discipline both sides and lecture them both so they don't do it again. Don Alejandro, on the other hand, encouraged them, saying,

> "Hug each other! Kiss each other!"
> —Alejandro Ardiles Caja

This worked, and they immediately made up. He also showed each child affection by always thinking about them and even creating a song for each. Each time he saw a child, he sang them their song.

César (4), Edith (10), and Carlos (3) in 1971 in Lima.

HOW HE RESPONDED TO TANTRUMS

Sometimes, one of his kids would get fussy. They might say "I don't like this food!" or "This soup is too hot!" and start crying.

Most parents would say, "Be quiet and eat!" but don Alejandro had another method. He took off his belt, but didn't use it to scare them. Cleverly, he would say, "The belt knows who's fussing," while holding it in front of each kid in turn. Finally, while laughing, he would say, "And the belt says…" and he would say the name of a kid who wasn't fussing. The one who was throwing a tantrum would start laughing thinking about the innocent one getting punished instead, and the fit would end.

HE TAUGHT HIS CHILDREN TO BE RESPONSIBLE

His son David, a manager of Siemens in Germany, remembers, "One morning in Quillcán, dad sent me to Pampas by horse to borrow his friend don Justino's crop sprayer. He told me to be quick because he needed to spray his potatoes. I was around eight or nine years old. When I got into town, I got distracted playing with my cousins, so I got the sprayer after lunch and went back to Quillcán.

Dad was outraged, and he fumed, 'You made me wait here all morning like a dawdler!'

It was getting dark after he sprayed his crops, and he made me take the sprayer back to Pampas on foot! The trek lasted several terrifying hours of stepping very carefully.

When I got back, I started thinking that I should have obeyed. I learned my lesson: be responsible. I never made that mistake again.

> "Behold, children are a heritage from the LORD,
> the fruit of the womb a reward."
> —Psalm 127:3

HE TRIED TO AVOID SAYING "NO"

These days, it's very common to tell kids, "I don't have time," or, "We don't have the money." Even though he had ten kids, Alejandro was always positive. He cleverly communicated the same thing in different terms. He would say, "We'll see."

"Dad, I have a field trip to Huancayo next week. I want to go."

"Sweetheart, there are a lot of accidents on those trips. The cars can turn over. It's better to be careful."

"Dad, I want to buy stylish pants."

"We'll see sweetheart."

"Dad, my throat hurts."

"Don't worry, it'll go away. Drink some lemon juice with honey."

"Dad, Peru is playing Brazil tonight in the stadium. We have to go."

"OK kids, we'll go."

HE HAD FAITH IN PEOPLE

DON SHESHA: A GREAT EXAMPLE

His ninth child, César, was difficult and belligerent in school, so they called his guardian. Don Alejandro was out of town, so doña Fortunata went instead. The teacher complained about César's bad behavior. Fortunata gave them permission to punish her son if it happened again. A week later, he got another citation. She went again and said, "I insist that you punish him if he misbehaves. I want him to straighten up!" She went home feeling embarrassed.

The next week, he got a third citation. This time, they made Alejandro come in to talk with the teacher. When he got home from school, all the kids were waiting to see his reaction, so César went and hid. What happened was the opposite of what they were thinking. When they asked what the teacher said about César, Alejandro said, "That don Shesha is the most obedient kid in school!" Everyone laughed--including César as he came out of his hiding place. From that point on, César straightened up and eventually became an international businessman.

HE LIMITED ELECTRONIC USAGE

Recent studies have shown that electronic devices—whether tablets, iPads, cell phones, or televisions—are harmful for children under two years of age due to the fact that they reduce attention span and real-world interaction and, over time, cause ADD, which is why human contact with family, friends, or parents is preferable.

Despite his poor education, Alejandro had all the newest gadgets in his house. However, he didn't buy a television when his kids were young so they wouldn't be distracted from their studies and they would develop a strong academic foundation. In doing so, he helped them avoid soap operas, violent shows, and other negative influences.

HE MADE TIME FOR EACH CHILD

The best thing a father can give his children is his time. Alejandro, in spite of his many jobs, always made time for each of his children.

His eighth child Edith, a current US resident, says, "When I enrolled in the Catholic university, I was able to play a lot of sports and compete in several championships. I remember when I ran in the university's marathon that they had every Thursday. Even though I was short, I wasn't intimidated at all. To get ready, I practiced every day with dad, who encouraged me constantly, saying that if I could run in Pampas Grande that I could definitely run in Lima.

"He was my biggest fan, and he cheered me on. 'Let's go chola! Let's go!' He clapped, laughed, and enjoyed it all as much as when I played soccer at the university. My athleticism undoubtedly comes from him."

HE TAUGHT HIS CHILDREN NEVER TO GIVE UP

His son Ángel remembers this story:

"When I was seventeen years old and my dad asked me what I wanted to study, I didn't hesitate in telling him 'Medicine.' He was shocked. It seemed as if he underestimated me.

'Medicine? You need fantastic grades to get in! Not even your sister Marcela with her Excellence Award has done that. You want to get in to San Marcos? Hmph!'

"To me, it was a challenge. I remembered that he had once told me that "A determined man never gives up! He meets his goals!' Six months later, he was the first to learn that I enrolled 25th out of 5,000 applicants to the San Marcos School of Medicine. Nobody knew about the personal challenge I had undertaken. I guess I learned his earlier lesson well!"

HE INSTILLED SELF-CONFIDENCE IN HIS CHILDREN

His daughter Julia recounts, "I could tell that the constant traveling to Pampas Grande to transport cattle and crops was wearing on my dad. One day, I thought, 'When dad gets old, he won't be able to go on like this. It's also very dangerous—he could hurt himself or get stranded along the route. I should do something to show him how much I love him and how thankful I am.'

"That's what pushed me to start a small business called 'Ferretería Ardiles,' where he worked driving truckloads of cement, propane, and various hardware paraphernalia until he was almost 80. Now, as an adult, I admire dad's attitude toward the challenge that I had undertaken with the hardware store. He wholeheartedly supported me economically and emotionally, which is the most important thing a parent can give to his or her children—self-confidence. When they discourage us, our morale goes down and we don't do anything. He encouraged me with his classic response: 'Ah, Julia Josefina!'

"Even though I am a woman and I didn't have any business acumen—much less in hardware—dad never discouraged me, which is why I had the honor of starting Ferretería Ardiles when I was 26 after graduating as an industrial engineer."

HE CORRECTED WISELY

César, his ninth child, says, "One memory from back then isn't so pleasant. I was managing Ferretería Ardiles, which my sister had founded. We had about $50,000 of capital. One night, there was a robbery that ruined us overnight. Eight years of hard work went down the drain. Dad was in the mountains at the time. I was upset, discouraged, and very afraid, because deep down I knew it was my fault for not securing the location. We lost everything. I thought dad would punish me for it, but the exact opposite happened. When he got back, I avoided him, but he came looking for me and said, 'Son, I was very poor when I was young. I never had anything, but I was able to advance in life through honesty, hard work, and faith in God. I'm old now, but you're young, and you have a lot of work to do.' That comforted me and gave me courage to keep pushing ahead. He taught me to keep a positive attitude when facing difficulties. When I was 26 years old, I took my first trips abroad. Dad was there to see me off and he always told me,

"Go with God and good judgment!"
—AAC

Don Alejandro wisely corrected his children because he based it on the Bible.

Edith, his youngest daughter, got married at the age of 34, and she was very attached to her parents. Her husband, Jehiel Aguilar, was a petroleum engineer and worked at the branch of Baker Hughes in Iquitos[20], Peru. Edith asked her father for advice:

"Dad, I don't want to go to the jungle. It's hot and there are mosquitoes. I want to stay near you in Lima. Do you think it's okay if I don't go to Iquitos?"

Don Alejandro told her, "Sweetheart, even though I would love for you to stay in Lima, you should be with your husband. You have to go to Iquitos."

> "So they are no longer two but one flesh."
> —Matthew 19:6a

HE NEVER LIED TO HIS CHILDREN

> "Never deceive a child. If you do, you're teaching him to be a liar. No matter how insignificant the promise, keep it."
> —AAC

One time, don Alejandro and his family gathered in the Jorge Chávez airport to say goodbye to aunt Edith before she went to Iquitos. Christian Daniel, his three-year-old grandson, wanted to go with her because he had never flown before.

"We'll go to Iquitos some other day," said his father. "You're a little too young."

---

20 Iquitos is the largest Peruvian city on the Amazon river

Don Alejandro with three of his daughters: Elena, Edith, and Julia.

A few weeks passed and Christian Daniel asked his father, "When are we going to Iquitos?"

His father got uneasy because he was an executive at the phone company and didn't have time to travel.

When don Alejandro realized what had happened, he said, "Never deceive a child. Let's go Christian! I'm taking you to Iquitos. Your dad doesn't have time."

And so, he took him.

HE INDULGED HIS CHILDREN

One day, don Alejandro noticed that his grandson Beremiz, his son Alex's son, was getting spoiled and didn't want to eat lunch. First, he wanted his parents to buy him pizza and a guarana soda, but his parents wanted it the other way around—first lunch, then the reward.

Don Alejandro wisely said, "You have to indulge your children. Buy him what he wants, then he'll eat in peace." He was right.

A LEADER SEES THE BEST IN HIS CHILDREN

Alejandro's dedication to his work grew every day just like his family. God rewarded him with ten children throughout his life. They were being born every two years—the first nine in Pampas Grande and the last in Lima—and they made a big, happy family.

There was nothing that motivated him more than his family. He and his wife helped their children to go far in life by giving them strong principles and values and a leadership mentality. Family is the most basic social unit and our main source of interactions.

He fostered a healthy home environment for his children's development. From the time they were little, they were his greatest treasure. As they grew, they also became his greatest source of pride, which is why he didn't spare anything in giving them the best nourishment possible.

According to a Global Home Index report, spending time with family contributes to better emotional, social, and psychological health. The quality is more important than quantity—even if you only have a few minutes, share some time with your family free from the distractions of phones and work. Being a good leader, he saw his kids' potential rather than their flaws and always focused on the positives. A leader creates new leaders, and that's what Alejandro did.

Following these pieces of advice, he got to see his children's accomplishments:

- Marcela: Studied biology and education at the National University of San Marcos. Former Director of the Esther Festini School in Lima.

- Ángel: Nephrologist at the National University of San Marcos. Studied medicine at Methodist Dallas Medical Center, Texas, United States.

- Elena: Studied social work at the University of San Martín de Porres. Master's degree in Social Projects at the National University of San Marcos.

- Alejandro: Studied petroleum engineering at the National University of Engineering. Worked as Drilling Manager of the Occidental Petroleum Corporation (OXY). Master's degree in business administration from the Pontifical Catholic University of Peru.

- Julia: Studied industrial engineering at the National University of San Marcos. Founder of the NGO Pan Peru. Co-founder of Autoespar and Grifos Espinoza. Director of Grupo Empresarial Espinoza S.A.

- Bernabé: Studied mechanical-electric engineering at the National University of Engineering. Master's Degree in Business Administration from the Peruvian Pacific University.

- Edith: Studied petroleum engineering at the National University of Engineering. Worked at Midland College as a teacher of GED courses in Texas.

- David: Studied electronic engineering at the National University of engineering. Winner of a scholarship to study electronic engineering in Germany. Currently works at Siemens in Nuremberg, Germany.

- César: Former student of the National University of Mining Engineering. CEO of his own company, Schubert Company.

- Carlos: Studied industrial engineering at the Pontifical Catholic University of Peru. Commercial Manager of Ardiles Import S.A.C.

Alejandro's ten children in his house in the Engineering District.

08

AN EXEMPLARY CITIZEN

A SERVANT

Don Alejandro had the gift of service for his community. Starting at five in the morning, the Pampas Grandes citizens would come to his house to ask him for favors and to give him letters and packages to take to Lima. Sometimes he had so many things to take that he would confuse them, lose them in his bag, or simply forget to take them. A month later, he would find them and deliver them like nothing had happened.

One day, they brought him three pumpkins to take to Lima. The road to Pariacoto was difficult on a pack animal, and the pumpkins were threatening to fall off. He got tired of having to situate them every few minutes, so he left them on the side of the road, bought three new pumpkins when he got to Lima, and delivered them with a smile.

HE DIDN'T MINCE WORDS

When people were doing bad things, he didn't mince words when correcting them—even if they were misbehaving authorities or teachers.

He would tell them, "What kind of example are you setting for your students shamelessly coming in here late and being a drunk?"

He also corrected the town drunks, who would often irresponsibly have ten or more children destined to be peons, saying, "You don't even have anything to eat and you're going to drink liquor?"

On the other hand, he publicly praised good. His reputation as an honest man had made him an authority, and everyone respected him and followed his advice.

HE GAVE BREAKFAST TO ORPHANS

"You're remembered not by what you get, but by what you give."

Every Mother's Day for more than twenty years, he threw a huge breakfast for the town's orphans and gave each one white flowers. He himself helped served the milk and warm bread rolls.

> "Whoever is generous to the poor lends to the Lord, and he will repay him for his deed."
> —Proverbs 19:17

AAC giving breakfast to the orphans.

Don Germán Aguilar Oncoy, Pampas Grandes' only tailor, remembers that "Don Alicho would leave the last two days of each harvest open for widows to come and take what they needed."

HE PROMOTED SOLIDARITY AFTER THE 1970 EARTHQUAKE

"Camaraderie will make greatness possible not only for Peru, but for all of humanity as well."
—José María Arguedas

After the 1970 earthquake, don Alejandro played an invaluable role. The 7.8 magnitude earthquake devastated the Andes, 70,000 people dying in less than five minutes. That Sunday, he was riding his horse to Pariacoto, Pampas' sister district, when the ground suddenly started shaking violently like it wanted to split the mountains, and the air went dark with dust.

When the earthquake passed, he noticed that his seven donkeys had died. He then had to decide whether to continue the journey to Lima where his wife and kids were waiting on him or to go back to Pampas Grande where the orphaned children of his sister Laura, who had recently died, were living. Amidst the pain, he thought, "In Lima, there are doctors, ambulances, and hospitals. In Pampas, there's nothing." He decided to return to Pampas to help.

On the way, he spread solidarity in the affected people by consoling, helping, and encouraging everyone he came across. When he arrived in Pampas, he shuddered upon seeing the rubble where the town used to be. The church and the Plaza de Armas—both colonial style architecture—were in ruins. Among the few buildings left standing were the

A house in Pampas Grande after the 1970 earthquake.

San Jerónimo school that he had built, his house, his late sister Laura's house, and a few others.

> "The angel of the LORD encamps around those who fear him, and delivers them."
> —Psalm 34:7

He immediately organized the people to bring aid to the injured and to get food. Fortunately, his nieces and nephews were unharmed, and he spent a few days with them. However, seeing the devastation, he decided to travel to Lima to get help for his village.

HE APPEARED ON TV AND THE COVER OF A MAGAZINE ASKING FOR AID FOR HIS VILLAGE

Don Alejandro appeared in the newspaper.

His cousin Manuel Castillo remembers, "I saw Alejandro—dirty and battered—arrive in Lima early one morning. He told me, 'Come on Channel 5 with me. I have to ask for aid for our town.' I told him, 'OK, I will, but get cleaned up first.' He said, 'No, I have to go like this so they'll believe me.' Incredibly, after he made a few arrangements, I was suddenly watching my cousin give his testimony on TV. He was very gutsy—he did everything he could to accomplish his goal."

He was bold, so he went to the biggest magazines and TV channels in the capital to tell them about the tragedy. He appeared on the cover of the Expreso magazine—one of the largest magazines in Peru—and on Panamericana Television Channel 5, where he said, "In my home town of Pampas Grande, bodies are lining the streets. We need food and medicine fast, because the children and elderly won't last much longer."

He returned to Pampas with truckloads of supplies, blankets, tents, and volunteers from Lima. The first helicopter ever in Pampas Grande arrived carrying North American aid workers.

Alejandro himself welcomed them with limited English, saying, "Goodbye, goodbye," instead of, "Welcome, welcome." The American volunteers smiled, understanding that the important thing was what he meant, not what he said.

HE BROUGHT TECHNOLOGICAL ADVANCEMENTS TO PAMPAS GRANDE

He always aimed to help his town develop technologically, which is why he immediately brought new devices back to Pampas from his trips to Lima, the United States, or Venezuela. He brought the first transistor radio—a Zenith—, the first TV, the first cellphone, and the first gas stove.

In 1978, his son Alejandro returned from Texas with a portable Panasonic radio/cassette player that also worked as a black and white TV. Don Alejandro, his son Bernabé, and his nephew Hugo Aguilar brought it to Pampas Grande to see if it would work.

First, they tried it in the sister districts Pira and Cajamarquilla without success. Then, they tried again in Pampas Grande. They were overjoyed when they saw the first images reach the little handheld device. The locals couldn't believe their eyes—TV in a town with no electricity or antennas!

Not even Huaraz, the capital of Ancash, had TV back then. It's understandable, then, that within ten minutes the entire town bustled with the news and crowded onto don Alejandro's porch. Many people watched TV for the first time that day. One 75-year-old woman said, "Now that I've watched TV in my own town, I can die in peace."

Later, they went to try the TV on the Quillcán estate where they even got to watch *The Incredible Hulk.*

This news was so shocking that it was even featured in the Lima paper *El Comercio*. A group of engineers from ElectroPerú was interested by the news and traveled to the village. Upon investigating, they determined that Pampas Grande's peculiar location acted as a huge parabolic antenna that captured TV signals as well as satellite signals. Amazingly, it even picked up radio signals from other countries!

Don Alejandro celebrated and said while laughing, "Canchón[21] is the world's antenna! Ha ha ha!"

---

21   The mountain on which Pampas Grande is located

HE EMPOWERED LOCAL FARMERS

Alejandro was never selfish—he always shared his farming and herding secrets with his Pampas Grande countrymen. He objectively and practically motivated and educated them regularly without incurring the theoretical distortions of the few agronomists and veterinarians who would later arrive in Pampas.

Don Luis Alegre Vega, a primary school teacher in Pampas Grande, sheds more light on details about this aspect of Alejandro's life. "By 1981, Alicho, then 63 years old, had 40 years of farming success under his belt. He always shared his knowledge and experience by giving practical education about growing potatoes and herding livestock. He was the opposite of selfish—sharing his experience with future generations. We should all be like that: the older generation teaching the younger."

He once offered a free district-wide educational session. There was major participation from the nine villages, who learned about topics like distancing between plants and rows, how long to wait before hilling, flowering, when to hill for the last time, and applying fertilizers and pesticides. He motivated each farmer to be entrepreneurial and independent instead of day-laborers with no purchasing power.

Ever since the sixties, he was fighting to get agriculture the well-deserved attention that it receives in more developed countries.

HE UNITED TWO TOWNS

For more than 300 years, Huanchay and Pampas Grande—neighboring districts—suffered from border disputes. Huanchay claimed—without basis—ownership of the peak of Canchón, the region's tallest mountain, in Pampas Grande.

Hoping to resolve this pointless dispute, Huanchay and Pampas Grande authorities met to discuss the issue. After two hours, instead of being closer to a solution, they were about to come to blows.

In this context, Alejandro, despite his old age, gave a memorable speech that would end the dispute and unite the two towns.

After hearing the speech, the authorities of the two towns signed a peace treaty and hugged as a symbol of unity—an historic and spiritual milestone that has lasted to the present.

> "The tongue of the wise commends knowledge…"
> —Proverbs 15:2a

The majestic peak of Canchón.

HIS FAMOUS SPEECH

"Representatives of Pampas Grande and Huanchay,

In spite of my old age, my poor health, and having not received an invitation to this meeting, I've come to contribute my small part to the benefit of these two towns.

My neighbors, my countrymen, and my brothers—both by geography and history—let there be no more fighting in the 20th century! Let's aim for peace, integration, and development. Let's fight to unite our paths to leave better towns for our future generations—the great men of tomorrow who will one day follow in our footsteps. We have to work together to overcome poverty!

Our children must live in better conditions than we do! So, let's stop fighting over a landmark and work together for a better and brighter future.

Thank you."

HE PROMOTED LOVE FOR HIS HOMELAND

"Never forget your parents or your homeland."
—AAC

His son Alejandro "Nuna" spoiled him just like don Alejandro had done to him when he was younger. Back then, Alex was already a petroleum engineer making good money at OXY, and he took his dad to different US cities. One time, he took him to Mérida, Venezuela, where he saw all the modern commodities of big cities in mountain houses, which motivated him to modernize his Pampas Grande house.

When construction started, the whole town thought he had gone crazy. Even his kids were uncomfortable with the massive cost. Everyone thought that nobody—not even his kids—would ever travel to Pampas Grande and that he was wasting the money because they had already lived in Lima for 30 years. Laughing, he said, "You all will see when I'm done! Ha ha ha!"

He was optimistic in a way that only he could be. He brought nice materials (bricks, cement, iron) and several bricklayers from Lima in his own trucks to build his dream house. It was modern, with electric lighting, water, sewer, heated baths, a built-in kitchen, face brick, and stone walkways. His dream came true in 1988. The brand-new house was the most modern on the entire Cordillera Negra of the Andes. Surrounded by his ten children and with tears in his eyes, he excitedly said the following:

"My dear children, never forget your parents or your homeland. No matter where you are, always come back and visit it. I dedicate this new house with its modern commodities to you and your future generations—that you might know the land of your ancestors. This house is here so that my grandchildren, my great-grandchildren, and tourists from all around the world can visit Pampas Grande, climb Canchón, and look at the sea and the sky as if from a balcony—all without lacking anything from the cities."

Incredibly, his dream is still a reality. His 39 grandchildren and 13 great-grandchildren—Peruvians, Germans, Americans, and Argentinians—have visited Pampas Grande and stayed comfortably in the house of their visionary grandfather.

Additionally, the Pan Perú Cultural Association for Childhood Aid has used that house since 2006 to host Peruvian and foreign volunteers and important figures such as doctors Rick Mayes, Sean McKenna, Sean Byrne, Sid Dante, Paula Tamashiro, and Emily Peron from the University of Richmond and Virginia Commonwealth University. They have traveled for more than ten years in a row with students and professionals to work to improve childhood health and education in Pampas Grande.

> "Put simply, my father was a visionary!"
> —His son Alex

Alejandro Ardiles' grandchildren (left) and great-grandchildren (right).

The house that don Alejandro built, which still houses the new generations in his family.

HE PROMOTED THE CONSTRUCTION OF THE HIGHWAY BETWEEN PAMPAS AND LIMA

When he was old, he often said, "I won't rest until my eyes see this highway to the coast get finished. Going to Pampas Grande through Huaraz and the mountains and ravines is hard, but the terrain through Huarmey, Culebras, and Huanchay is gentle like taking an escalator."

Holding to the belief that "better communication means better development," he completed his last project to help his village by managing the construction of a new highway that connected Huarmey/Culebras with Huanchay, Pampas Grande, Cajamarquilla, Pira, Yupash, and Huaraz. He worked with the Ministry of Transportation and Communication as a simple citizen and indefatigable proponent of progress, not a political figure. Today, this highway is one of the four connecting routes between the coastal towns and the mountain towns of Ancash.

He didn't rest until the leg of the highway between Pampas Grande and Huanchay, a project which was abandoned for 30 years, was finished. He even used his own money to speed up the process and encouraged people to lend a hand.

When he was 83 years old and in poor health, he finally saw his dream come true. On January 13, 2001, in the presence of the president of the Ancash Regional Administration Transitory Council (CTAR), agricultural engineer José Narváez Soto, and a delegation of the Lima Pampas Grande Social Club, an excited don Alejandro sponsored the opening of the road that would unite four Ancash districts from his wheelchair.

> "Fame comes and goes, but greatness lasts forever."
> —Anonymous

Opening of the Yupash-Culebras highway with his cousin Lucas Castillo, 2001.

09
FINAL GOODBYES

On March 10, 2009, surrounded by his ten children Marcela, Ángel, Elena, Alejandro, Julia, Bernabé, Edith, David, César, and Carlos and his dear wife Victoria Fortunate, Alejandro Ardiles Caja passed away in Lima, Peru.

FUNERAL EULOGY TO DON ALEJANDRO ON THE DAY OF HIS PASSING, MARCH 12, 2009

You set an example of love—with your children, your close family, the needy, and, in particular, your beloved Pampas Grande. How could we forget that even after a massive stroke, hardly able to stand, you wanted to manage the construction of the Yupash-Culebras highway—the project you dreamed about? You wanted us to take you in your wheelchair when it was opened, and you saw your countrymen dance for joy.

How could we forget your love for your children? Each night, you got home from work and gave us all a group hug. You could carry almost all of us at the same time, and you sang us each the song you had written for us.

How could we forget how you demanded that we hug and kiss each other to make up after each and every fight? You were a fierce protector of children, orphans, widows, and the elderly. The few Sundays you had off, you went to the town and shared lunch with them and freely gave them part of your harvest.

You also set an example of education in spite of the fact that you hardly received one. You closely monitored the teachers of both boys and girls by visiting classrooms and assessing the students' progress. We will always remember your vision of education—bringing your children, nieces, and nephews not to Huaraz or Chimbote, but straight to Lima—and how you prepared your little children to be competitive, saying, "Be brave! You're Peruvian!"

You taught us about management and leadership. Motivated by your calling to education, you mobilized your village by going from household to household, motivating them to build a school in Pampas Grande—your greatest and most unprecedented project that you completed without funding from the City Council. (We know you were using your own money and telling the people that the Ministry was sending part.) Amazed, I watched you start that project one Sunday in the Plaza de Armas when you called people together. They thought it would be a dedication of the first stone like the authorities often do. Instead, we started laying the foundations for the classrooms and the different households were competing, the women were preparing food for the workers, and the band that played on Sundays was livening up the atmosphere.

You simultaneously managed several businesses, protecting your employees of each one and organizing your nightly soccer games with your Petromax lamps. Matará vs. San Juan. You made UDP, your own soccer team, as well as FC Ardiles with your sons.

You taught us a timeless lesson about values with your well-known phrase, "Don't steal, don't lie, don't be lazy," which you faithfully exemplified. You demanded fulfillment of promises and made a ranking of the representatives of those values from the town.

You imparted your success to your children, nieces, and nephews, and you built your house near the University of Engineering because you wanted your children to become engineers. Your vision came true—seven of your children are engineers and the others are doctors.

Thank you, dad. You fulfilled your purposes in life to the letter. I carry your teachings in my veins, and my nine siblings and I promise to take care of mom and to stay together. I repeat: one day we'll see each other again and we'll enjoy your presence and your teachings in eternity. See you later, dad.

Your oldest son, Doctor Ángel Ardiles

10
ALEJANDRO ARDILES CAJA'S MASSIVE LEGACY

ALEJANDRO ARDILES CAJA'S LEGACY

The Bible says,

"Blessed is everyone who fears the Lord, who walks in his ways! You shall eat the fruit of the labor of your hands; you shall be blessed, and it shall be well with you. Your wife will be like a fruitful vine within your house; your children will be like olive shoots around your table. Behold, thus shall the man be blessed who fears the Lord."

—Psalm 128:1-4

My dear reader, if we're faithful to him, God fulfills what he promises in his scriptures just like he did with don Alejandro, who, in spite of growing up in abject poverty as an orphaned peasant farmer with hardly any education, kept a positive attitude like a beautiful carnation growing in the middle of a desert.

Instead of falling into self-pity, discouragement, or depression, he trusted in the Lord and worked vigorously and honestly. The only one he feared was the Lord, whom he loved and respected throughout his life.

This is exactly why he had a happy and successful life. His slogan was, "Go with God and good judgment!"

He led a balanced life free of excess because all excess is evil.

Thanks to his identity in God, he succeeded in all areas of his life. Monetarily, he became the best farmer and breeder the Cordillera Negra of the Andes had ever seen. In his family, he created unity. Spiritually, he kept his heart close to God. Socially, he was loved and appreciated by all. Politically, he served as governor and mayor without pay.

I have witnessed his happiness. The phrase, "with Christ, every home is a happy one" came true in his family. The world needs happy people and families, and more than simple knowledge is needed for that. It takes daily transformation based on the Word of God.

So take a moment to reflect. Reflection is a state of mind where one truly examines their thoughts and words. Then, you recognize the errors and shortcomings that we all have. The key is repentance (true change and true forgiveness) followed by restoration, which leads to unity and harmony.

Close your eyes, give your heart to God, and these things will be added unto you. Dare to be happy!

Keep loving. Keep helping. Keep sharing. Keep growing.

Julia Ardiles de Espinoza

APPENDICES

ARDILES ANICETO FAMILY TREE

The first Ardileses came to Peru from Argentina. Some stayed in Puno, others in Arequipa, and a few kept going toward Pachacamac, Lima. These would eventually go to Huarmey, Ancash and up into the Andes until they settled in the Alley of Huaylas and its surrounding areas.

José Ardiles, who was from the Alley of Huaylas, married Beatriz Milla from Huarmey.

Their child, José Eladio Ardiles Milla, married Elisa Robles, a teacher from Aija.

They decided to live in Pampas Grande where they would found the estate called "Quillcán" in San Juan, El Dorado.

José Eladio Ardiles' and Elisa Robles' nine children and their grandchildren are as follows:

1. **Trifonio Ardiles Robles:** Clara, Felícita, Esther, Vilelmina, and Edelmira.
2. **Juan Ardiles Robles:** Juan, Iberón, Elisa, and Socorro
3. **Julio Ardiles Robles:** Teobaldo, Áurea, Alejandro, José, Melitón, Magdalena, Natalia, Fortunato, Dictinio or Cristóbal, and Sócrates.

4. **Antonina Ardiles Robles:** Graciela and Zoraida.

5. **Beatriz Ardiles Robles:** Gustavo, Rolando, Augusto, Lucas, Maruja, Manuel, and Guillermo.

6. **Alejandrina Ardiles Robles:** Rebeca, Carlos, Adolfo, and Humbertina.

7. **Bernabé Ardiles Robles:** Alejandro, Laura and Antoinette.

8. **Alejandro Ardiles Robles:** None

9. **Laura Ardiles Oaks:** None

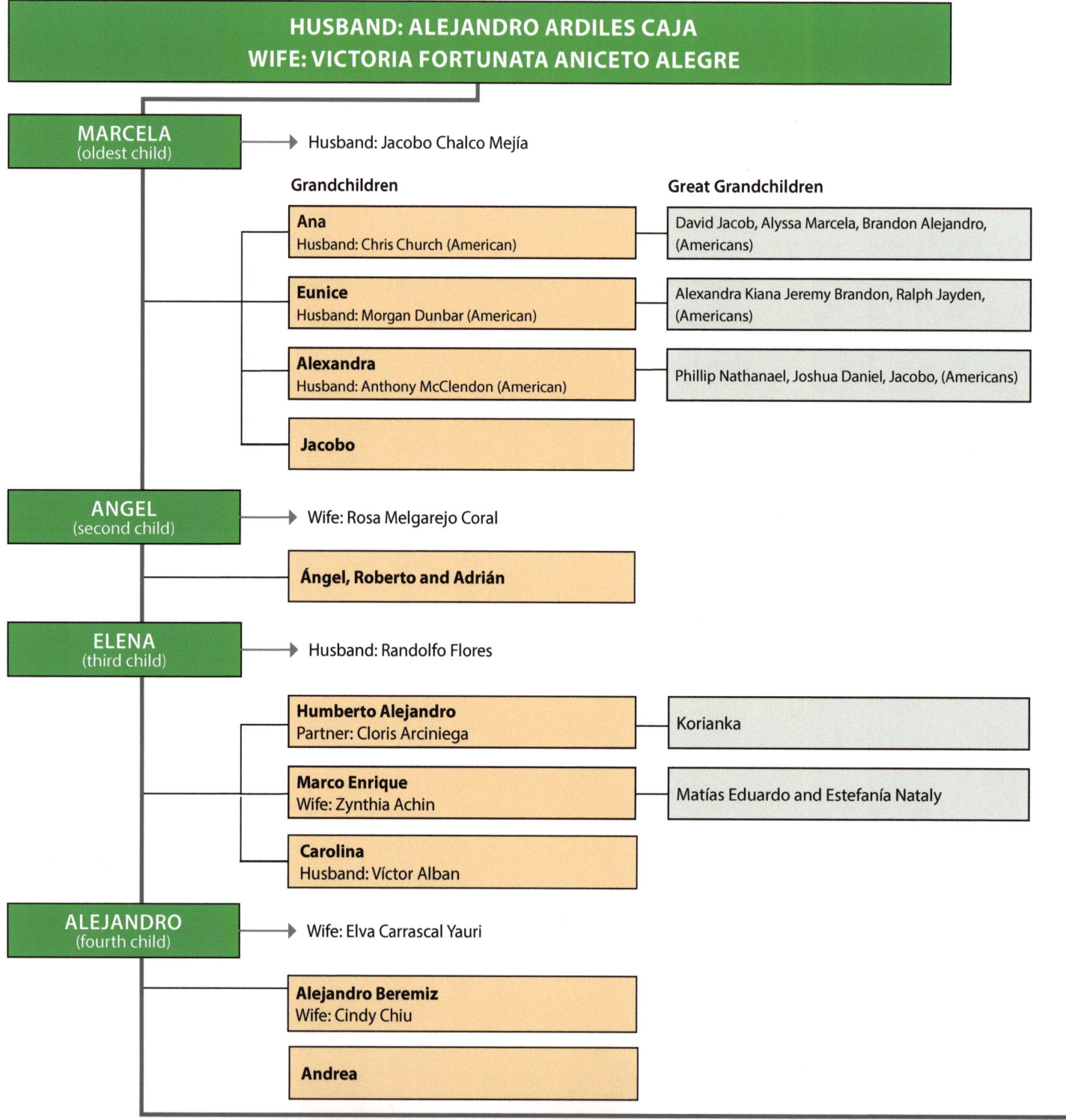

JULIA ARDILES DE ESPINOZA

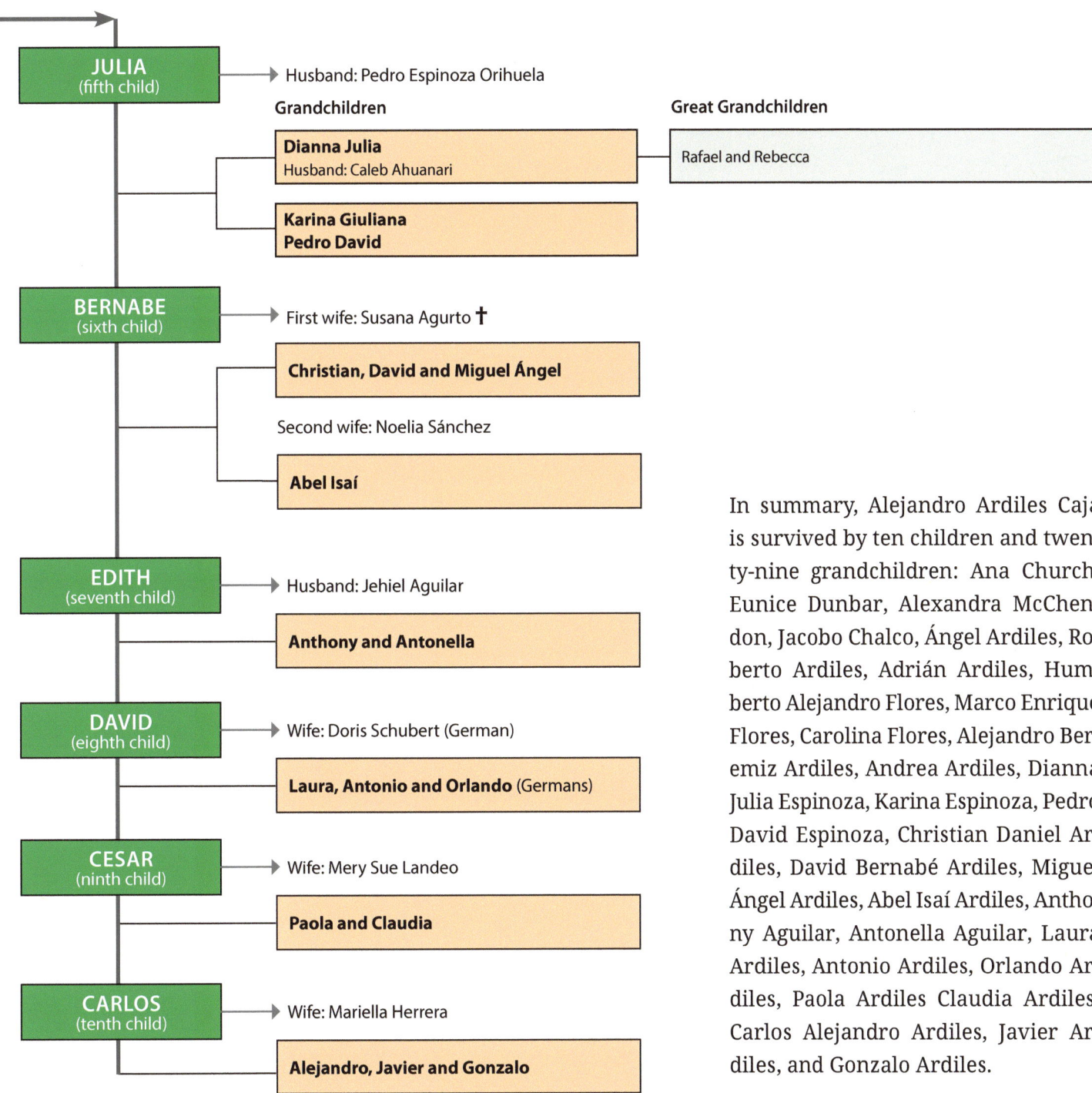

In summary, Alejandro Ardiles Caja is survived by ten children and twenty-nine grandchildren: Ana Church, Eunice Dunbar, Alexandra McChendon, Jacobo Chalco, Ángel Ardiles, Roberto Ardiles, Adrián Ardiles, Humberto Alejandro Flores, Marco Enrique Flores, Carolina Flores, Alejandro Beremiz Ardiles, Andrea Ardiles, Dianna Julia Espinoza, Karina Espinoza, Pedro David Espinoza, Christian Daniel Ardiles, David Bernabé Ardiles, Miguel Ángel Ardiles, Abel Isaí Ardiles, Anthony Aguilar, Antonella Aguilar, Laura Ardiles, Antonio Ardiles, Orlando Ardiles, Paola Ardiles Claudia Ardiles, Carlos Alejandro Ardiles, Javier Ardiles, and Gonzalo Ardiles.

TESTIMONY OF HIS CHILDREN

Biologist and Educator

National University of San Marcos. Former director of the Esther Festini School in Lima. United States citizen. Latina women's ministry leader at the Crieve Hall Church of Christ in Nashville, Tennessee.

Dad, you were a wonderful child of God. Your exemplary life taught us to love our families, our cherished Peru, and all of humanity, but most importantly, you taught us to believe in God.

My dad accompanied me in the most special moments of my life. When I had to take an admissions test to get into the Lima Elvira García y García school, dad tirelessly encouraged me until—thank God—I was accepted. I finished the school year with good grades, and he excitedly told me, "You make me look good, sweetheart!" He never stopped lifting my spirits, and his constant encouragement made me get better every year.

The day of my admissions test for the National University of San Marcos, he took the bus with me, gave me an extra pencil, and encouraged me with his usual, "Sweetheart, go with God!"

I thank God for having given me such a wonderful, loving, and dedicated father. Thank you, dad—Alejandro. One day, we'll be together in heaven forever.

Ángel

Nephrologist

National University of San Marcos. Head Physician at Rebagliati Hospital—the best public hospital in Peru. Soccer player for San Fernando College of Medicine soccer team. Completed a Fellowship at the Methodist Dallas Medical Center.

As his oldest son, I got to share my entire childhood, adolescence, and adulthood with my dad, as well as part of my middle age. I can confidently say that he was a major influence of my personal and professional development.

My father wisely guided me in life, so I consider myself to have inherited his success. I've been able to apply his wise counsel, values, and examples in every aspect of my life, and I believe that who I am today is a product of his daily instruction.

He was a spiritually and emotionally balanced and constantly positive man. He wanted to serve his town, he taught by example, and he fiercely opposed indecency, lying, and stealing. He was a natural athlete—just as good at basketball as he was at soccer—with a joyful disposition, and he was mischievous and strong. He devoted himself to his work and knew how to make time to celebrate with his family. At parties, he was constantly dancing and having fun.

Elena

Social worker
University of San Martín de Porres. Master's in Social Projects from the National University of San Marcos. Worked at multinational nonprofits such as World Vision and Every Child.

The thing I remember most about my father is his love and commitment to his family and children. I also remember his optimism, self-confidence, leadership, ability to influence, dedication to good, and his tireless fight to help both us and Pampas Grande keep moving forward.

It makes me happy to remember his joy on so many occasions, like when my sister Marcela received the Excellence Award after finishing high school at Elvira García y García, when my brother Bernabé enrolled in the National University of Engineering in first place, when my brother Alex traveled to the US for the first time shortly after graduating, or when dad went with Edith to her soccer championships at the Pontifical Catholic University of Peru.

However, the most important thing I can stress about him is his ability to organize and lead projects to improve the lives of his children and his people.

Despite his early setbacks, he became an exceptional father and exemplary citizen that, with only two short terms as mayor of Pampas Grande, managed to create the first secondary school and the most important highway for our village. In summary, he was a loving father, a tireless fighter, and a model citizen.

Alejandro

Petroleum Engineer

National University of Engineering. MBA from the Pontifical Catholic University of Peru. Former Senior Drilling Manager of the Occidental Petroleum Corporation (OXY). Former president of the Peruvian-Venezuelan Cultural Center in Maracaibo, Venezuela. President and Founder of Ardiles Import S.A.C.

My father always pushed us toward personal, professional, and social success, and I've applied his wise teaching in every aspect of my personal life. He was, put simply, a visionary.

I'm sure that everyone can be successful, good people and good professionals. They just need to trust in God and have the will to study, overcome, make their dreams a reality, and look for ways to make the world a better place.

Julia

Industrial Engineer

National University of San Marcos. Founder of Ferretería Ardiles. Founder of Pan Peru — a 501(c)3 nonprofit organization that empowers underserved children and women. Co-founder of Toyota Autoespar (Toyota Dealer), and Grifos Espinoza GESA (Primax Dealer) in Peru. Board Member at Grupo Empresarial Espinoza. Author of "Uncle Rabbit" and "El Tío Conejo".

There's always a person in someone's life that acts as a cornerstone. For me, that was my father. I've never met a man more positive, dedicated, courageous, optimistic, honorable, hard-working, generous, intelligent, enthusiastic, humorous, or capable of facing the life's challenges with confidence and the desire to make all his friends and family happy.

Remembering him, I wish I could shout, "I love my dad!" from a mountaintop.

I love my father so much because he was my friend, my companion, my constant encourager, and my dance partner. For years, I proudly walked with his constant support. "Ah, Julia Josefina!" was his classic greeting every time he saw me and wrapped me in his arms.

My father's vision to modernize his Pampas Grande house in 1982 was admirable. Years later, that house became the headquarters of the NGO Pan Perú and the place where international volunteers dedicated to making the lives of local children better stay. Through Pan Peru, I followed his footsteps and made my dream come true: building the first modern library in rural Peru.

Bernabé

Mechatronic Engineer
National University of Engineering. MBA at Universidad del Pacífico. Former manager of the Peruvian phone company. Finances manager at Ardiles Import.

I've spent a lot of time with my dad in my life. During my school breaks, we traveled from Lima to Quillcán to work in the fields and with the livestock where I observed firsthand his ability and leadership in managing businesses.

I helped him buy his Hillman car in 1973 and his Dodge 300 truck in 1974. First, I was his assistant, then his driver. We went between Pampas Grande and Lima often.

It's hard to find people like my dad—honest, hard-working, smart, brave, strong, responsible, loving to his people and family, generous to the needy, a visionary, and an excellent leader.

I thank God for giving me an extraordinary father. I don't think that even dad recognized some of his own accomplishments because they were just part of his mental framework. For him, working and succeeding were natural. His hard work and sacrifice were the cost of the example, education, and professionalism that he left his children.

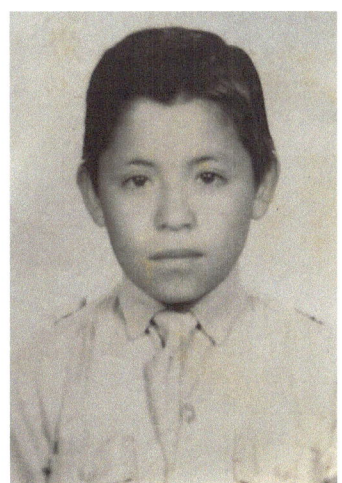

Thank you, dad. Thank you, mom—his loving wife. Without your support, none of his accomplishments would have been possible.

Edith

Petroleum Engineer
National University of Engineering. United States Resident. Worked as a teacher of GED courses at Midland College in Texas.

When I talk about dad, I think about what he taught us—love for people, sharing, helping the needy, being brave, and so much more. I think the best way to honor his memory is to put those lessons into practice.

For example, helping out our family and spending time together so the next generations keep that love and unity—even with cousins, nieces, nephews, and other relatives.

When I enrolled at the Pontifical Catholic University of Peru, I was able to play a lot of sports and compete in several championships. I remember when I ran in the university's marathon that they had every Thursday. Even though I was short, I wasn't intimidated at all. To get ready, I practiced with dad every day, who encouraged me constantly, saying that if I could run in Pampas Grande that I could definitely run in Lima.

He was my biggest fan, and he cheered me on. "Let's go chola! Let's go!" He clapped, laughed, and enjoyed it all as much as when I played soccer at the university. My athleticism undoubtedly comes from him.

Even though he didn't know how to drive very well, he took me in his car to school. He was loving, and I admire that he always made time to encourage and support his children.

David

Electrical Engineer

National University of Engineering. Won a scholarship to study electrical engineering in Germany. German citizen. Current sales manager of Siemens in Erlangen, Germany. Former president of the Peruvian Cultural Association in Munich, Germany.

When I was in the National University of Engineering, there were frequent strikes, which meant no classes. During those times, I had to go with dad to Pampas Grande, Quillcán, and the other places he went to do business.

I had applied for a scholarship offered by INABEC to study in Germany. There were about three thousand applicants and five positions. During the process, we had to take a lot of tests. When it was down to 150 finalists, INABEC let the Germans themselves decide who would go.

We were in Quillcán at the time and I was feeling discouraged because my classmates had told me that the scholarships were always rigged and that I shouldn't get my hopes up. In my heart of hearts, I wanted the scholarship to open up doors for my future, but everything pointed to me not winning.

Early one morning, my dad got up and told me, "Son, I had a dream: you're going to Germany." That gave me hope, and I thanked God for the encouragement. Finally, the dream came true.

Up till this day, my biggest motivation is the memories I have of my dad. He inspires me to keep pushing forward to my goals.

César

Mining Engineer

National University of Engineering. Well-known imports businessman. Founder of CEAR-DISA, F&A Company and Schubert Company. Chairman & President of Schubert Company.

One day, I woke up from a deep sleep in our Quillcán house. My brother Alejandro was next to me. We had traveled together from Lima to see the final touches being put on the new house and to play soccer in Pampas Grande for our beloved San Juan Team.

With tears in my eyes, I managed to breathe and ask God to help me survive the 12,500-feet altitude at Pampas. At 2:00PM, we started the game against our rival: Matará. Given that I was 42 years old, it was a great day for me when I scored three goals in the official match. I was excited because I ran all 90 minutes without crumbling from fatigue.

Deep down, I was upset about my father's irremediable absence. I instinctively looked for him in the stand—especially when I scored. A whisper from heaven calmed me down and a voice told me, "It's OK, don Shesha!" like my dad always called me. Even though he wasn't there physically, his voice echoed in my heart and mind.

I remembered how, when I was a kid, my dad would leave the house in Lima to go to his cherished Pampas Grande. My sisters would take me to the store to buy candy so I didn't have to watch him leave. When I got back home and I couldn't find him, I would begin to cry inconsolably and get so upset that I would kick the wooden doors until I broke them. If there's one thing I never understood, it's why God didn't allow me to be born earlier so I could spend more time with my father and give him back a portion of what he gave me. He was, without a doubt, guiding my life with his example and his advice.

Industrial Engineer

Pontifical Catholic University of Peru. Commercial Manager of Ardiles Import S.A.C. Soccer striker.

Writing about my dear father fills me with melancholy for his absence, with emotion for his example, and with pride for his spiritual greatness. I thank God for letting me be a part of his family—his youngest child!

Alejandro was a talented, dynamic, dedicated, athletic, strong, and energetic man. He planned ever more difficult goals and objectives in life, but he always accomplished them.

He would then share the benefits of those successes with his loved ones, his family, his friends, and the less fortunate, showing his heart's greatness.

When I was born, he was fifty. He was always with me on the special moments in life, from the first day of primary school to the last day of high school.

One March 10th, he left us. Ten like the number of the soccer stars that he admired. A ten that shines now amongst millions of stars.

If it's worth anything, I ask for his forgiveness for the many times I took advantage of his great love, and I am eternally grateful to God for the time I shared with my father.

TESTIMONY OF HIS FAMILY AND FRIENDS

Karina (granddaughter)

Pediatrician Resident at Children's Hospital of Orange County in California. Stanford University Class of 2012, bachelor of arts in human biology. Virginia Commonwealth University School of Medicine Class of 2019, Doctor of Medicine.

My grandfather Alejandro Ardiles was very important to me. He always told me, "Karina, the three most important things you should learn are, 'Ama llulla, ama quella, and ama sua,'" which means, "Don't be a liar, don't be lazy, and don't be a thief" in Quechua.

I remember how much he liked to sing and play cards. When I lost as a little girl, I would get mad and cry; however, he didn't let me win because he wanted to teach me that there are winners and losers in life. His story was impressive. As a child, he was an orphan living in the Andes. With just a few years of schooling, he became the mayor of Pampas Grande and helped widows and poor kids.

Unfortunately, I was in the US at Stanford when he passed away, and I didn't get to tell him goodbye. Whenever I think of him, I hope to become more like him: brave, generous, and honest.

Ana Church (granddaughter)

Graduated from Lipscomb University in Tennessee with a degree in business administration.

The thing I most admired about my grandfather was his constant effort to unify his family. It seems like yesterday when we all met Sunday after Sunday at Cervatel's recreation center in Santa Clara—children, grandchildren, in-laws, nieces and nephews, and neighbors—to play sports together.

Many people knew our family and would say to us, "You guys are a remarkable family because you're unified." That's his greatest legacy—uniting us through good times and bad.

He knew how to engender love among his children and family. There's no doubt that we've always dearly loved one other.

Beremiz Ardiles (grandson)

Graduated from the University of Pennsylvania with a degree in economics

The thing I most admired about my grandfather Alejandro was his strength, leadership, and dedication to his work, but also his love and care for his large family. He was a brave, just, generous, and big-hearted man. He was strict when necessary, but he also knew how to make life better with his great sense of humor and love for dancing. He was a great dancer!

We spent so many great evenings playing cards together! I think his greatest legacy is having taught his children and grandchildren that hard work and perseverance can produce great results.

Román Yauri Ardiles (nephew)

United States resident

I get excited when I remember uncle Alejandro. At the age of eight, I moved in with him after my father Braulio passed away in 1948, leaving my mother with four children. There aren't many uncles like that. He and my aunt Fortunata, who is like a second mother to me, took us in and supported us.

His example taught me three valuable lessons: wake early, be hard-working, and be honest. Now, I apply them in New Jersey where I live as a US citizen.

Inocencia Villafuerte Colonia

Former mayor of Pampas Grande

Don Alejandro taught many Pampas Grande citizens his methods, from preparing the land to selling products and getting better prices. Many citizens are thankful for his teaching and advice.

Cancio Valverde Ardiles

Former Pampas Grande alderman

Uncle Alejandro was the main driver of the Pampas Grande-Huancay highway, which is now one of the main connecting routes between the coastal towns and the mountain towns of Ancash. As mayor, he worked in conjunction with his aldermen to preserve and improve the ponds, passages, and horse trails in each of the district's sectors.

He was an excellent farmer, growing grains and potatoes in quantities unlike any other Pampas Grande citizen. The mountain and coastal markets were saturated, so he took his products to Tarapoto, San Martin, in the jungle to get better prices. Uncle Alejandro was also the district president of the Nicolás Trinidad Rojas Agrarian Directors Association—a position he successfully and enthusiastically filled. He supported breeders and farmers so they could produce more and encouraged them to secure loans from the Agrarian Bank of Peru. In doing so, he benefited all the local citizens with his work.

Victoriano Tolentino Colestino

Director of the Pampas Grande National School of San Jerónimo

The only thing Alejandro Ardiles Caja deserves is our thanks for his excellent work in the interest of Pampas Grande—especially for the School of San Jerónimo, which was realized through his work and leadership. His works will continue to grow like Canchón's shadow with the setting of the sun.

Adolfo Fournier Ardiles (cousin)

Former Peruvian Army Major

I like talking about Alejandro, or, as his family lovingly called him, "el Ñato" or "el Chato." Thinking about him, I remember a visionary who knew how to influence everyone around him.

One rainy evening in the February on 1948, Alejandro arrived in Quillcán. The year before, we had finished primary school in Pampas Grande and many of the locals had already gone to Huaraz to prepare to enroll in the National La Libertad high school. That evening, Alejandro told me, "Ponash [that's what el Ñato called me], you have to go to Huaraz to enroll in La Libertad. There's no reason for you not to have a career and you have the opportunity to study. Don't you want to join the military? I brought two horses to take you."

Six years later, I enrolled in the Chorrillos Military School in Lima. Alejandro congratulated me as if I were his son. The same thing happened when I graduated as a second lieutenant. We celebrated with a hearty hug and we shed a few tears in memory of my parents, who had passed away while I was in school and were not able to see me become an official in the Peruvian Army.

Alejandro made a permanent impact on me and I still admire him greatly.

STORIES

Alejandro Ardiles Caja was humorous, cheerful, jocular, and a joker. He had a great memory for jokes and stories.

To preserve his laughter in our memories, we've recorded some of the funny stories that he frequently told below.

THE PERFECT RETRACING

One day, don Alejandro made a spur of the moment decision, like he often did, to travel to Pampas Grande. His wife ran to buy cakes and prepare his clothes, saddlebags, and other things that he always brought.

When he was ready to leave, he couldn't find his keys.

Becoming somewhat distressed, he looked around for them. "Darn! I'm getting forgetful! I know I just had them…"

His son Alex suggested, "Dad, calm down and retrace your steps. You'll find them."

"OK, OK."

He grabbed a keyring and started to retrace his steps. Suddenly, he realized he had lost the new bunch of keys only God knows where.

Everyone laughed when my brother told him, "Dad, you retraced your steps perfectly!"

DON NOVATO CANO

One of his best friends was Don Novato Cano, a renowned teacher in Pampas and the Director of the 335 Boys School.

One day, don Novato traveled to Cuzco to see Macchu Picchu. He was tall, white, bulky, and handsome, so some tourist mistook him for a gringo and asked him if he spoke English. He only spoke Spanish and Quechua, so he obviously didn't understand. However, he didn't hesitate to respond in Quechua, saying, "Cam no, noca pizentiendichu," which means, "Like you, I don't understand a thing." The American became worried thinking that don Novato had been speaking in Russian.

Back then, there was a fierce rivalry between the US and Russia.

Don Alejandro often jokingly told this story of how his great friend had spooked an American tourist.

CRASHING HIS TRUCK

One day, he let me borrow his blue Mazda pickup. I was young, but already married. When I left the bank, I wrecked the truck.

I know it was my fault, but I'm not lying when I say that the breaks were slow and that it didn't stop when I braked. They hit me hard enough on the driver's side that I couldn't open the dented door.

When my dad got there, he didn't hound me at all. There was nothing about women drivers or worrying about the repairs. Instead, he asked me, "Sweetheart, are you OK?"

"I'm OK dad," I responded.

"Ah, Julia Josefina! Ha ha ha. Don't worry about it. What's important is that you're OK. Keep driving."

LOOKING FOR A JOB

Marcela successfully finished simultaneous degrees in biology and education at the University of San Marcos. Strangely, she couldn't find work in Lima due to "not being qualified."

One day, don Alejandro saw that she was concerned and told her, "Go to Pampas Grande and work there. All my relatives are authority figures, and you'll easily find a job."

She responded, "No, dad. You can't even wear heels in Pampas Grande. Everything rugged and uneven."

So he told her, "That doesn't matter sweetheart. We can tell Mamerto to carry you around in a wheelbarrow," and everyone laughed at the idea.

DON GERMÁN IN THE AIRPLANE

Don Germán, Alejandro's brother-in-law, who had always lived in Pampas Grande, went to New Jersey. He was happy to visit his kids in the US for the first and to have seen New York. Everything seemed great to him, but he commented that the winter was even worse than in Pampas.

When he left the house to return to Pampas with his grandson Edgar, he was wrapped up with a scarf, cap, and coat like Santa Claus. On the plane, Edgar noticed that his grandfather was sweating in the heated cabin, pointed the air at him, and said, "Grandpa, you're sweating. Take your jacket off."

Don Germán responded, "You're right. Thankfully, someone opened the windows—I'm catching a little breeze."

HIS NEPHEW "ACHISITO"

His nephew Diómedes—a cheerful, white-skinned, green-eyed boy—was nicknamed "Achisito." He and another white boy were coming from Huaraz to Pampas, but they ran out of money halfway. They got hungry, so they came up with the idea to pretend to be American tourists in the nearby town Pira.

Achisito told his friend, "I'll do the talking. You stay quiet."

It was nighttime, so they went to the Pira police station and spoke to the supervisors in the most gringo Spanish they could muster. "Nosotros no hablar spanish, solo english. Nosotros ir Pampas Grande [We no speak Spanish. Only English. We go Pampas Grande]."

They signed that they were hungry and tired.

"Nosotros tener hambre [We hungry]," while they signed like they were eating.

"Tener sueño [We sleepy]," while they laid their heads in their hands.

"Ayudar please [Help, por favor]," putting their hands together to beg.

The policemen believed them and told themselves, "These poor tourists are lost." They immediately helped them, giving them good food and beds.

Early the next morning, the commissioner came to review the previous night's happenings. When they told them about the American tourists going to Pampas, he was very curious and wanted to meet them because he was from Pampas.

Naturally, he was surprised to find out that they were imposters. As a punishment, he made them sweep the Pira Plaza de Armas to teach them not to lie again.

PHOTOGRAPHS

The beautiful flowers—called Sutoc Marias—in Pampas Grande.

Don Alejandro's vast property in Pampas Grande.

Don Alejandro and doña Fortunata surrounded by their children.

A group of students and teachers with RGHA (USA) who traveled to Pampas for social work in collaboration with the NGO "PAN PERU" and who stayed in the house that don Alejandro built.

Pedro Espinoza, his daughter Elena, his niece Elena Valenzuela, Manuel and André Rios, and his children César, Julia, and David.

Don Alejandro and his daughter Julia in San Francisco. Left: at the Golden Gate Bridge. Right: in the city's trolleys.

Don Alejandro with his cousins Guillermo and Manuel Castillo.

Don Alejandro with his niece Conie and his cousins Juan, Felicita, and Edelmira.

Don Alejandro with his cousins Adolfo Fournier and Guillermo Castillo.

[Left to right] Don Alejandro; his children Elena and Bernabé; his daughter-in-law Rosa; his children Ángel, Alejandro, Marcela, and David; his wife doña Fortunata; his granddaughter Carolina; and his children Edith, César, Carlos, and Julia.

His sons César and David with his wife doña Fortunata in Germany.

Family picnics with his wife, children, grandchildren, and nieces and nephews.

His son-in-law Pedro, his children David and Julia, his granddaughter Laura, his daughter-in-law Doris, and his grandchildren Karina, Dianna, Pedro David, Antonio, and Orlando in London.

His nieces and nephews—his sister Antonieta's children—Elena, Eduardo and Bety Valenzuela with his daughter Julia.

His daughter Julia with her nuclear family.

His grandchildren Paola, Pedro David, and Claudia with his son, César.

His children Carlos and Julia.

His cousin Manuel Castillo with his daughter Julia.

His son Alejandro; his daughter-in-law Elva Carrascal; his grandchildren Marco Enrique, Zintya, and Pedro David; his brother-in-law Randolfo Flores; his daughter Elena; and his granddaughter Andrea.

Reynaldo Trinidad Ardiles—one of his closest and most loved nephews.

PHOTOGRAPHS

His daughters Marcela, Julia, Edith, and Elena.

His grandson Christian Daniel, his son Bernabé, his daughters-in-law Susana and Elva, his granddaughter Carolina, his daughters Julia and Edith, and his grandsons Beremiz and Marco Enrique.

His daughter Edith in the United States.

His children Julia and Carlos in his house in the Engineering District.

His ten children with his wife doña Fortunata.

Don Alejandro with his children Carlos and Edith, his brother-in-law Jehiel Aguilar, his daughter Julia, and his wife doña Fortunata.

His sons Ángel, Alex, Bernabé, David, César, Carlos.

Don Alejandro playing soccer with his sons.

His daughter Julia, who loves her country just like her father did.

His nieces and nephews Clementina Ardiles, Guido Yauri, and Judith Aguilar and his daughters Julia and Edith.

His daughter Elena, Cesario Trinidad—husband of his cousin Lidia—, his niece Katia, his daughter Marcela, and his son-in-law Jacobo Chalco.

His grandchildren Pedro David, Anthony, and Karina; his son-in-law Jehiel Aguilar; and his daughter Edith and Julia.

Don Alejandro and his nieces Bety, Daysi, Dani, and Rosa.

His niece Susan Fiorita, don Porfirio, his sister Antonieta, and Robert Fiorito in New York.

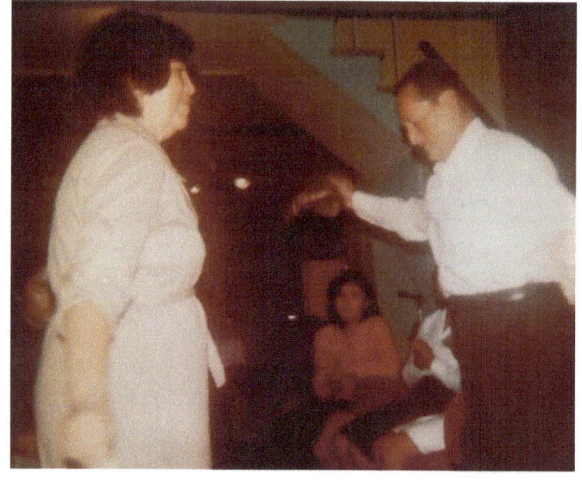

His beloved sister Antonieta and her husband don Porfirio dancing.

His sister Antonieta and don Porfirio.

His sister Antonieta and don Porfirio in the United States.

Julia Ardiles de Espinoza
is a devoted Christian, a graduate of the National University of San Marcos with a degree in industrial engineering, the founder of "Ardiles Hardware" and the NGO "PAN PERU—Cultural Association for Childhood Aid", and co-founder of Autoespar S.A. She is a licensed Toyota and Grifos Espinoza S.A. dealer in Peru as well as a Primax dealer and CEO of Grupo Empresarial Espinoza. She is the author of the storybook, "El Tío Conejo."

www.ingramcontent.com/pod-product-compliance
Lightning Source LLC
Chambersburg PA
CBHW041151290426
44108CB00002B/40